1981 Biennial Exhibition

Whitney Museum
of American Art

1981 Biennial Exhibition
Whitney Museum of American Art

Fourth floor: January 20–April 5, 1981
Third floor: January 27–April 19, 1981
Second floor: February 4–April 12, 1981
Films, second-floor Film/Video Gallery: February 4–April 12, 1981
Video, second-floor back gallery: February 4–April 12, 1981

This exhibition is sponsored by the American Can Company Foundation. In addition, travel by curators was made possible by a grant from the National Endowment for the Arts.

ISBN 0-87427-032-4

This publication was organized at the Whitney Museum of American Art by Doris Palca, *Head, Publications and Sales*, Sheila Schwartz, *Editor*, James Leggio, *Copy Editor*, Anita Duquette, *Rights and Reproductions*, and Anne Munroe, *Assistant*.

Artists' Biographies were compiled by Caroline Angell and Karl Willers.

Designed by Bruce Campbell
Typeset by Elizabeth Typesetting Company
Printed by William J. Mack Company

Photograph Credits

Joel Breger (Fleischner), Geoffrey Clements (Benglis, Borofsky, Burton, Callis, Francisco, Friedman, Meyerowitz, Misrach, Ollman, J. Shapiro), Bevan Davies (Michals, Moskowitz, Rosenquist), D. James Dee (Efrat, Kushner, MacConnel, Schnabel, Wegman), Jonathan Dent (Jensen), eeva-inkeri (Amenoff, Bailey, Downes, Garet, Murray, Price), Roy M. Elkind (Hunt, Keister, Robbins, Thorne), Rick Gardner (Bartlett), Bill Giduz (Warren), Bruce C. Jones (de Kooning), Julius Kozlowski (Pfaff), Kevin Noble (Sigler), Douglas Parker (Smith), Eric Pollitzer (Jenney, Paschke), Robert Reck (Thompson), © Steven Sloman (Porter, J. Snyder), Steven Sloman (Held), Nathaniel Tilestone (Wilson), Thomas P. Vinetz (Arnoldi), © Wolfgang Volz (Christo, Morrel).

The American Can Company Foundation is proud to sponsor, along with the National Endowment for the Arts, the 1981 Biennial Exhibition of the Whitney Museum of American Art.

In joining the Whitney in its presentation of this outstanding exhibition of the most provocative and challenging works of contemporary artists, the American Can Company through its foundation is clearly demonstrating that its interest is focused on innovation and sustained achievement.

It is important to the American Can Company as a member of the business community to restate its recognition of the significance of art in enhancing our lives with its invention and diversity. The talented American artists whose works have been selected from all parts of the country for the Biennial bring promise and excitement to all of us.

William S. Woodside
Chairman
American Can Company

Foreword by the Director

The 1981 Biennial is the first exhibition to follow the celebration of the 50th Anniversary of the Whitney Museum of American Art. It reaffirms the dedication of the Museum to a tradition begun by its founder, Gertrude Vanderbilt Whitney, in 1932 of focusing on the achievements of living American artists on a regular basis.

The role the Whitney Museum plays in American art today is quite different from that conceived by its founder. Mrs. Whitney and Juliana Force, the first Director of the Museum, recognized a particular need that existed at the time of the founding of the Whitney Museum—to show the work of American artists and support them financially. The interest in and awareness of American art on the part of art and educational institutions and the public has broadened tremendously in the last fifty years. The Whitney Museum has played a vital role in this evolution, and today the Museum is an institution with a responsibility both to the public and to artists. Even amidst a greater appreciation of American art, criticism invariably descends upon the Biennial Exhibitions. Many institutions have abandoned large surveys of contemporary art, but the Whitney Museum has maintained its commitment to the Biennial as a statement about the art of our times.

It is extremely gratifying that this year a major grant from the American Can Company Foundation has assisted us in presenting the Biennial Exhibition. This support from an American corporation for one of the most controversial endeavors the Museum undertakes is commendable and identifies the American Can Company with some of the most creative artists of our times. The National Endowment for the Arts continues to support the travel programs of the curators, who make a considerable effort to view the work of artists throughout the United States.

This year, for the last time, the upper three floors of the Whitney Museum will be devoted to the Biennial Exhibition. Beginning in the fall of 1981, a permanent installation of outstanding works from the Permanent Collection will occupy the third floor, thereby removing it from use for temporary exhibitions. This installation of the Permanent Collection will identify the Museum with particular works on a continuing basis, and establish a selection of twentieth-century painting and sculpture which can act as a counterpoint to the temporary exhibition program. Even though considerable space will be devoted to the permanent installation, the commitment of the Whitney Museum to the Biennial and to the work of living artists remains at the center of its accomplishments.

Tom Armstrong

Preface by the Curators

Since their inception in 1932, the Whitney Museum Biennial Exhibitions have been among the most important surveys of contemporary American art. These exhibitions have continuously assessed the wide spectrum of current art; they were originally conceived, as Juliana Force wrote in the catalogue of the first Biennial, to "represent in a broad way some of the most notable characteristics of American [art] today." The 1981 Biennial Exhibition, like its predecessors, is a non-juried, invitational selection of some of the most provocative and accomplished work produced by American artists in the previous two years. It is not restricted only to young and unknown artists, but rather brings together new work by artists of all ages and stages of development.

The organization and presentation of the 1981 Biennial focuses on a number of the predominant attitudes, concerns, and modes of expression that engage contemporary American artists: an expressionistic and gestural approach to abstract painting; non-objective painting and sculpture based on formal, geometric configurations; painting and sculpture that explore various aspects of traditional realism; differing approaches to representation, including painting and sculpture that treat images as abstracted symbols, gestural depictions of representational subject matter, and figurative painting emphasizing a quasi-surreal narrative; objects that are amalgams of painting and sculpture; multi-media installations; and photography.

In addition, a slide presentation of large-scale outdoor sculpture constructed for specific sites allows this important aspect of recent art to be included within the format of the Biennial. As in previous years, the 1981 Biennial presents a selection of videotapes and films reflecting the important contributions made by artists working in these media, and focuses on artists outside the documentary and conventional narrative traditions. Whenever possible, more than one work by an artist is shown, and a number of works and installation pieces were made especially for this exhibition. By including the work of both established and lesser-known artists from throughout the United States, the exhibition is intended to provide a framework for better understanding the diverse creative vitality that characterizes the art of this period.

JOHN G. HANHARDT
BARBARA HASKELL
RICHARD MARSHALL
PATTERSON SIMS

Vito Acconci

Mobile Home, 1980
Mixed media, 8 x 8 x 16′
(2.4 x 2.4 x 4.8 m)
Sonnabend Gallery, New York

Sliding Doorway, 1980–81
Mixed media, 8 x 8 x 16′
(2.4 x 2.4 x 4.8 m) overall, open position
Max Protetch Gallery, New York

Robert Adams

Interstate 10, San Bernardino County, California, 1979

Eucalyptus, Riverside, California, 1979
Black-and-white photograph, gelatin silver print, 11⅛ x 8⅞" (28.2 x 22.6 cm)
Castelli Photographs, New York

Interstate 10, San Bernardino County, California, 1979
Black-and-white photograph, gelatin silver print, 8⅞ x 11⅛" (22.6 x 28.2 cm)
Castelli Photographs, New York

Redlands, California, 1979
Black-and-white photograph, gelatin silver print, 8⅞ x 11⅛" (22.6 x 28.2 cm)
Castelli Photographs, New York

Gregory Amenoff

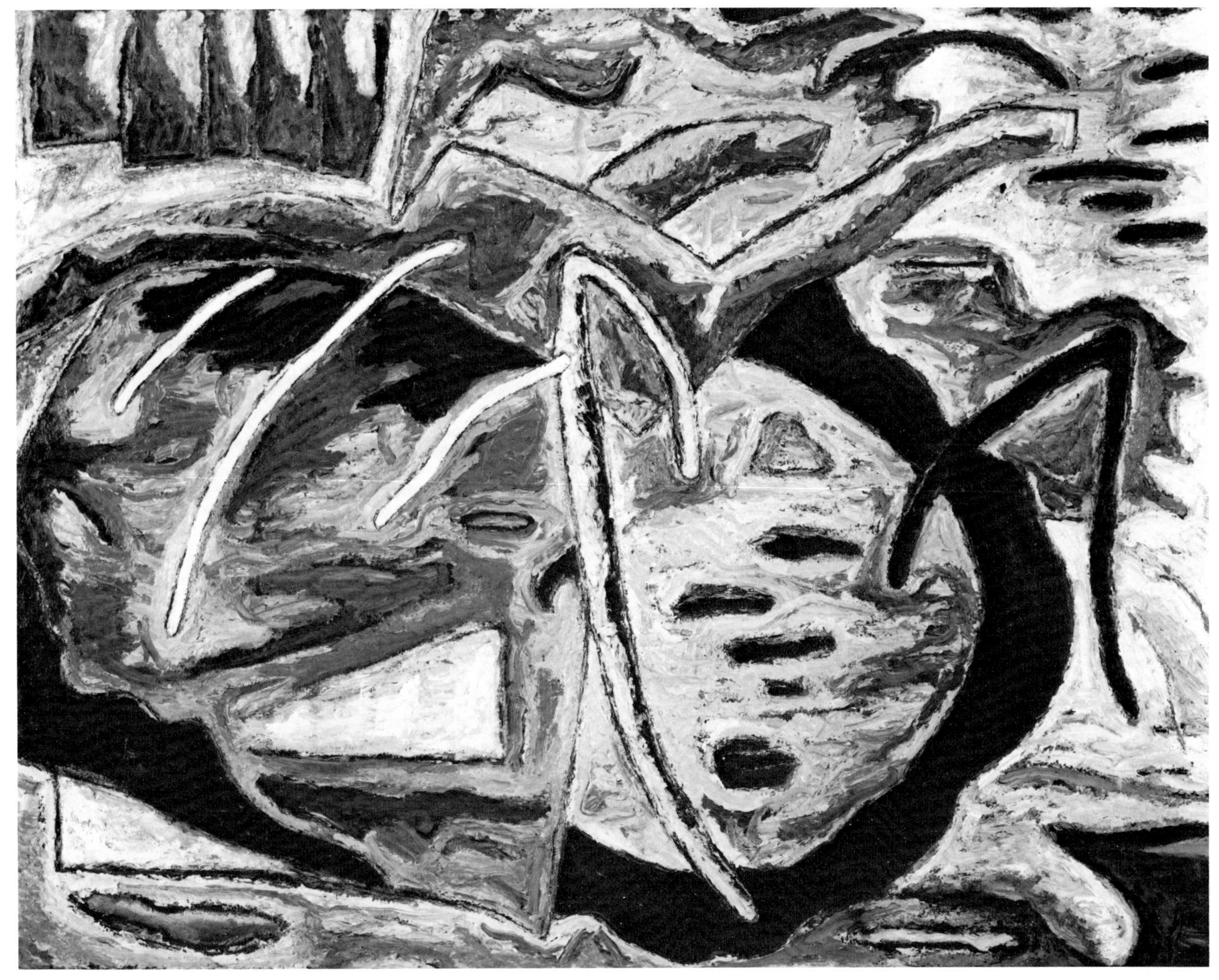

Overlook, 1980

Bayou Teche, 1980
Oil on canvas, 68 x 78″
(172.8 x 198.1 cm)
Collection of Graham Gund, courtesy
Nielsen Gallery, Boston

Overlook, 1980
Oil on canvas, 70 x 92″
(177.8 x 233.8 cm)
Collection of Martina Hamilton, courtesy
Robert Miller Gallery, New York

William Anastasi

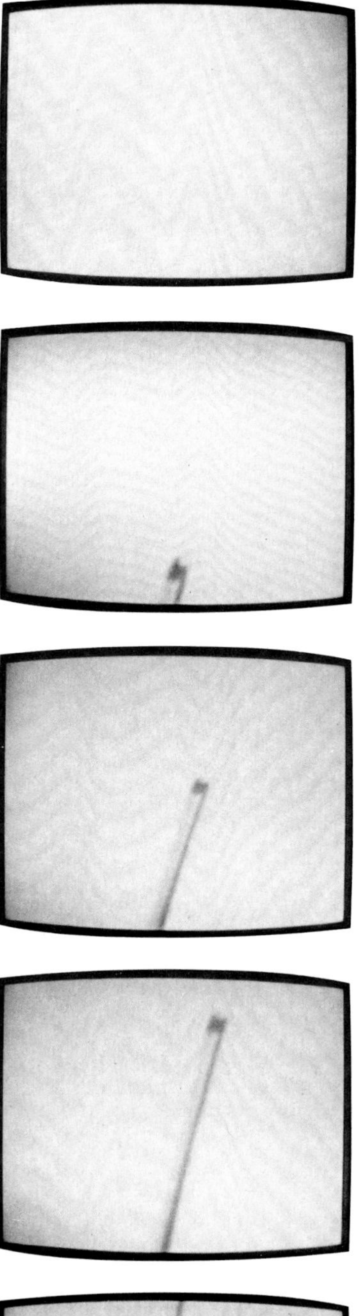

Zukovsky's Bow, 1979

Zukovsky's Bow, 1979
Video, black and white, 36 minutes
Lent by the artist

Video Program V
Wednesday, February 4–Sunday,
April 12, daily at 2:30, Tuesdays at 7:00

Kenneth Anger

Still from *Lucifer Rising*, 1980

Lucifer Rising, 1980
Film, color, 30 minutes
The American Federation of Arts, New York

Film Program V
Tuesday, March 10–Thursday, March 26, daily at 1:15; Tuesday, March 10, and Tuesday, March 24, at 6:00

Siah Armajani

Reading Garden #3, 1980

Slide presentation of the following works:

Fifth Bridge, 1979
Wood and steel, 12 x 90 x 36′
(3.6 x 27 x 10.8 m)
Installation for Wave Hill, Bronx, New York

Reading House, 1979–80
Painted wood, 16 x 32 x 22′
(4.8 x 9.6 x 6.6 m)
Installation for XIII Winter Olympic Games, Lake Placid, New York

Reading Garden #3, 1980
Painted wood, 11 x 57 x 30′
(3.3 x 17.1 x 9 m)
Installation for Neuberger Museum, State University of New York, College at Purchase

Charles Arnoldi

Untitled, 1980

Untitled, 1980
Oil on tree branches, 96 x 96 x 96″
(243.8 x 243.8 x 243.8 cm)
Collection of Laura-Lee Woods

Alice Aycock

The Large Scale Dis/Integration of Micro-Electronic Memories, 1980

Slide presentation of the following works:

From the Series Entitled How to Catch and Manufacture Ghosts: Collected Ghost Stories from the Workhouse, 1980
Galvanized steel, steel, wood, glass, birds, motors, approximately 30 x 60 x 80′ (9 x 18 x 24 m) overall
Installation for the University of South Florida, Tampa

The Game of Fliers, 1980
Wood, steel, cable, fire, water, birds, approximately 45 x 100 x 25′ (13.5 x 30 x 7.5 m) overall
Installation for 12th and G Streets, Washington, D.C.

The Large Scale Dis/Integration of Micro-Electronic Memories, 1980
Wood, approximately 18 x 200 x 150′ (5.4 x 60 x 45 m) overall
Installation for Battery Park City Landfill, West and Chambers Streets, New York

William Bailey

Manhattan Still Life, 1980

Manhattan Still Life, 1980
Oil on canvas, 40 x 50″ (101.6 x 127 cm)
General Mills Collection, Minneapolis, Minnesota

Still Life with Speckled Bowl, 1980
Oil on canvas, 40 x 50″ (101.6 x 127 cm)
Robert Schoelkopf Gallery, Ltd., New York

Jennifer Bartlett

Sunrise, Sunset II, 1979

Sunrise, Sunset II, 1979
Enamel, silkscreen grid, baked enamel
on steel plates and oil on canvas,
approximately 12 x 12′ (3.6 x 3.6 m)
Paula Cooper Gallery, New York

Water at Sunset, Swimmers at Sunrise, 1979
Oil on canvas, enamel, silkscreen grid
and baked enamel on steel plates,
approximately 12 x 12′ (3.6 x 3.6 m)
Paula Cooper Gallery, New York

Lynda Benglis

Eclosion Grouping, 1980

Eclosion Grouping:

Maya (Illusion), 1980
Brass screen, hydrocal, gesso, gold leaf,
45½ x 10 x 11″ (114.3 x 25.4 x 27.9 cm)
Private collection

Amboda (Flounce), 1980
Brass screen, hydrocal, gesso, gold leaf,
23½ x 25½ x 11⁵⁄₁₆″
(59.6 x 64.8 x 28.7 cm)
Paula Cooper Gallery, New York

Kaya (Body), 1980
Brass screen, hydrocal, gesso, gold leaf,
25 x 25 x 9⅞″ (63.5 x 63.5 x 24.8 cm)
Paula Cooper Gallery, New York

Pankh (Wing), 1980
Brass screen, hydrocal, gesso, gold leaf,
49⅛ x 9½ x 11⅜″
(124.5 x 24.6 x 28.6 cm)
Collection of Mr. and Mrs. Robert S. Hillman

Mattha (Head), 1980
Brass screen, hydrocal, gesso, gold leaf,
27¼ x 16⅜ x 13¾″
(69.2 x 41.2 x 34.9 cm)
Paula Cooper Gallery, New York

James Benning

Still from *Grand Opera,* 1979

Grand Opera, 1979
Film, color, 90 minutes
Lent by the artist

Film Program IV
Friday, February 20–Sunday, March 8,
daily at 3:15; Tuesday, March 3, at 6:00

Jonathan Borofsky

Installation at Paula Cooper Gallery, New York, November, 1980

Installation, 1981
Mixed media
Lent by the artist, courtesy Paula Cooper Gallery, New York

Stan Brakhage

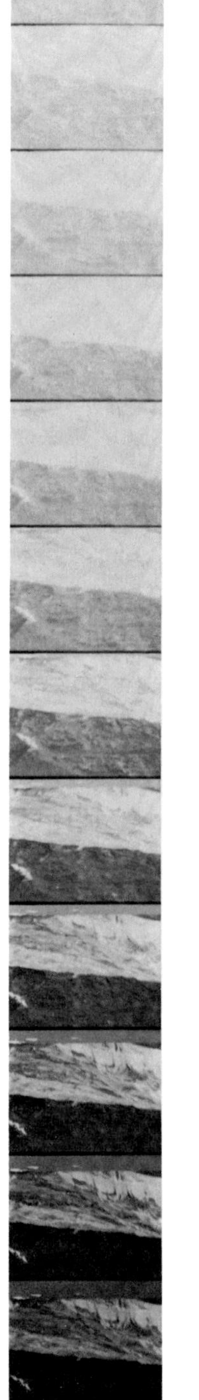

Frames from *Creation,* 1979

Creation, 1979
Film, color, 10 minutes
Filmmakers Cooperative, New York

Other, 1980
Film, color, 3 minutes
Filmmakers Cooperative, New York

Film Program I
Wednesday, February 4–Thursday, February 19, daily at 1:15; Tuesday, February 10, at 6:00

Robert Breer

Frames from *T.Z.*, 1979

T.Z., 1979
Film, color, 9 minutes
Lent by the artist

Film Program III
Friday, February 20–Sunday, March 8, daily at 1:15; Tuesday, February 24, at 6:00

Michael Brewster

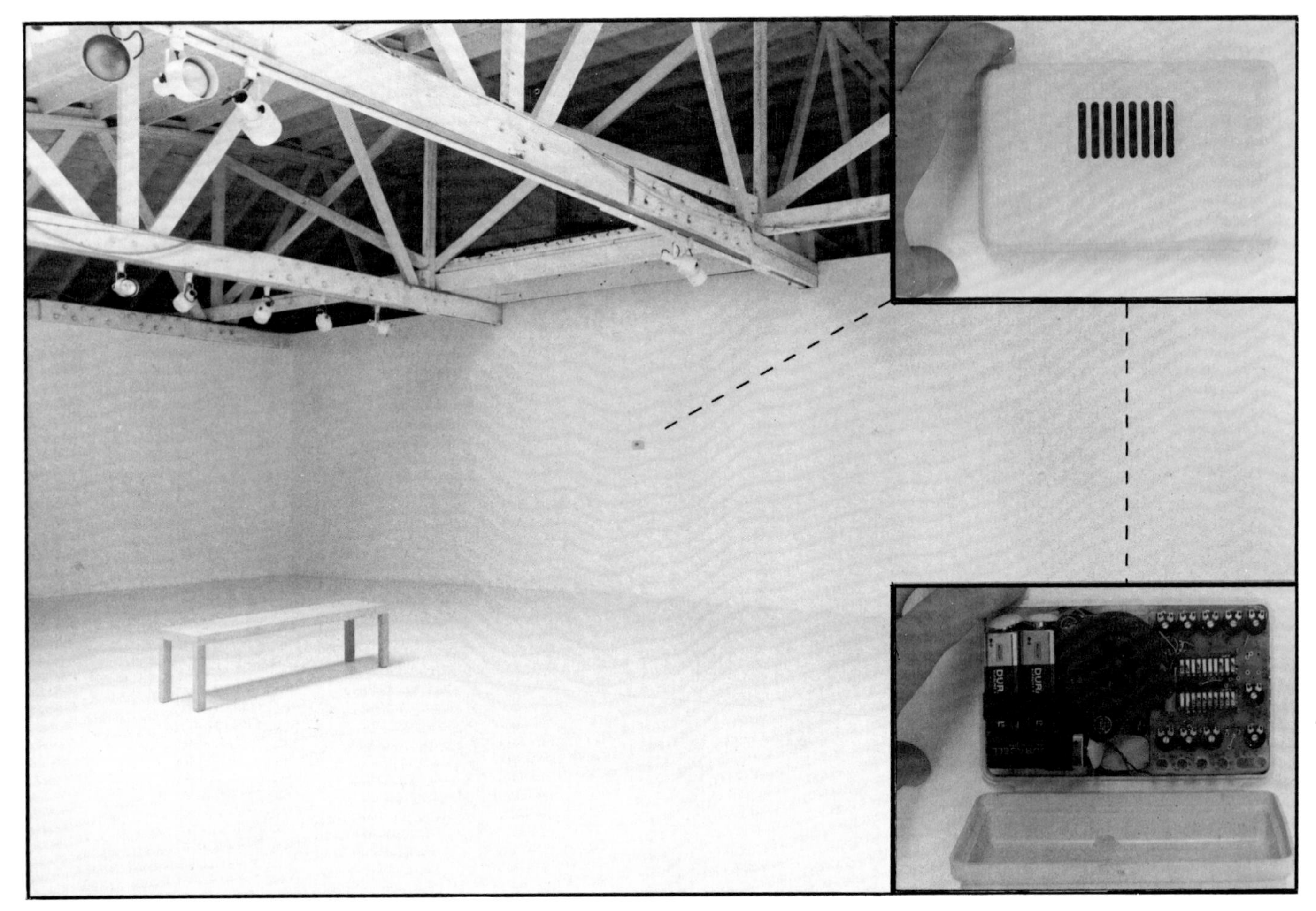

Surrounded: Sharp Points Ringing, 1979
Installation with close-up details of sound-generating device, *The Multi*
Cirrus Gallery, Los Angeles

Echocentric (An Acoustic Sculpture), 1981
Installation with electronic sound-generating device
Lent by the artist

Barbara Buckner

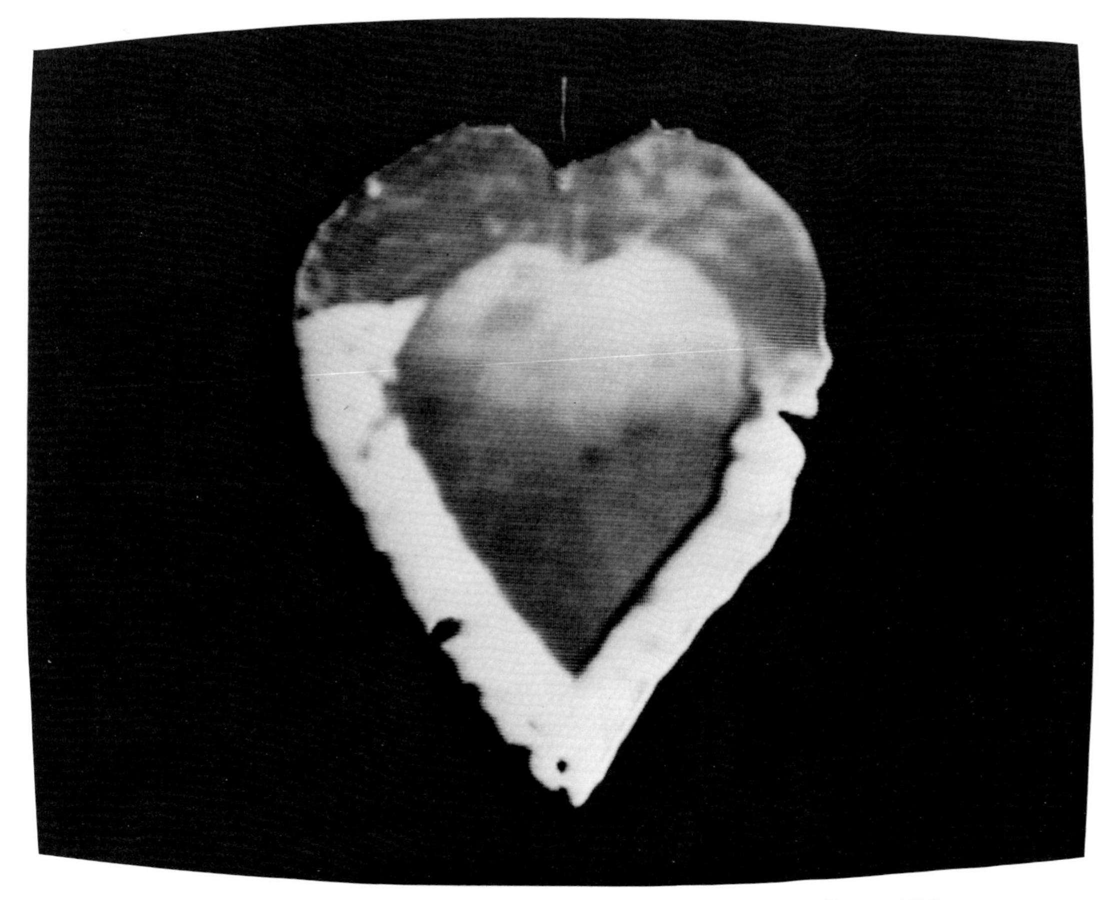

Hearts, 1979

Hearts, 1979
Video, color, 12 minutes
Lent by the artist

Video Program V
Wednesday, February 4–Sunday, April 12, daily at 2:30, Tuesdays at 7:00

Scott Burton

Study for *Chair and Table* (Rock-Furniture Series), 1980
Painted papier-mâché, 3¼ x 3½ x 3½ (8.3 x 8.9 x 8.9 cm) and 1¾ x 2¼ x 2¼" (4.5 x 5.7 x 5.7 cm)
Collection of the artist

Table, 1978–81
Onyx, steel armature, fluorescent and incandescent lights, 29 x 60 x 60" (73.7 x 152.4 x 152.4 cm)
Max Protetch Gallery, New York

Two Chairs (Rock-Furniture Series), 1980
Granite, approximately 36 x 40 x 40" (91.4 x 101.6 x 101.6 cm) each
Max Protetch Gallery, New York

Harry Callahan

Ireland, 1979 © Harry Callahan

Calais, Maine, 1979
Color photograph, dye-transfer print,
10¼ x 15⅝" (26 x 39.5 cm)
Light Gallery, New York

Cape Cod, 1979
Color photograph, dye-transfer print,
10¾ x 15¾" (27.3 x 40 cm)
Light Gallery, New York

Ireland, 1979
Color photograph, dye-transfer print,
7¼ x 10⅝" (18.4 x 26.8 cm)
Light Gallery, New York

Ireland, 1979
Color photograph, dye-transfer print,
7 1/16 x 10½" (18.1 x 26.7 cm)
Light Gallery, New York

Jo Ann Callis

Salt, Pepper, and Fire, 1980

Parrot and Sailboat, 1980
Color photograph, Cibachrome print,
20 x 24″ (50.8 x 61 cm)
G. Ray Hawkins Gallery, Los Angeles

Salt, Pepper, and Fire, 1980
Color photograph, Cibachrome print,
24 x 20″ (61 x 50.8 cm)
G. Ray Hawkins Gallery, Los Angeles

Spaghetti and Mashed Potatoes, 1980
Color photograph, Cibachrome print,
20 x 24″ (50.8 x 61 cm)
G. Ray Hawkins Gallery, Los Angeles

Louisa Chase

Ravine, 1980

Ravine, 1980
Oil on canvas, 72 x 96″
(182.9 x 243.8 cm)
Private collection, courtesy Robert
Miller Gallery, New York

Thicket, 1980
Oil on canvas, 70 x 90″ (177.8 x 228.6 cm)
Private collection

Christo

Wrapped Walk Ways, Loose Park, Kansas City, Missouri, 1977-78

Slide presentation of the following works:

Wrapped Walk Ways, Loose Park, Kansas City, Missouri, 1977–78
Woven nylon cloth and mixed media,
14,000 yd^2 (12,000 m^2) of fabric over
2.7 mi (4.5 km) of park walkways

The Mastaba of Abu Dhabi Project for the United Arab Emirates (proposal) 1977–
390,500 stacked oil barrels,
492 x 338 x 984′
(147.6 x 101.4 x 294.6 m)

Larry Clark

Untitled, from *42nd St.*, 1979

Untitled, from *42nd St.*, 1979
Black-and-white photograph, gelatin silver print, 8½ x 12⅜" (21.5 x 31 cm)
Lent by the artist, courtesy Robert Freidus Gallery, New York

Untitled, from *42nd St.*, 1979
Black-and-white photograph, gelatin silver print, 12⅜ x 8½" (31 x 21.5 cm)
Lent by the artist, courtesy Robert Freidus Gallery, New York

Untitled, from *42nd St.*, 1979
Black-and-white photograph, gelatin silver print, 12⅜ x 8½" (31 x 21.5 cm)
Lent by the artist, courtesy Robert Freidus Gallery, New York

Untitled, from *42nd St.*, 1979
Black-and-white photograph, gelatin silver print, 12⅜ x 8½" (31 x 21.5 cm)
Lent by the artist, courtesy Robert Freidus Gallery, New York

Untitled, from *42nd St.*, 1979
Black-and-white photograph, gelatin silver print, 12⅜ x 8½" (31 x 21.5 cm)
Lent by the artist, courtesy Robert Freidus Gallery, New York

Robert Cumming

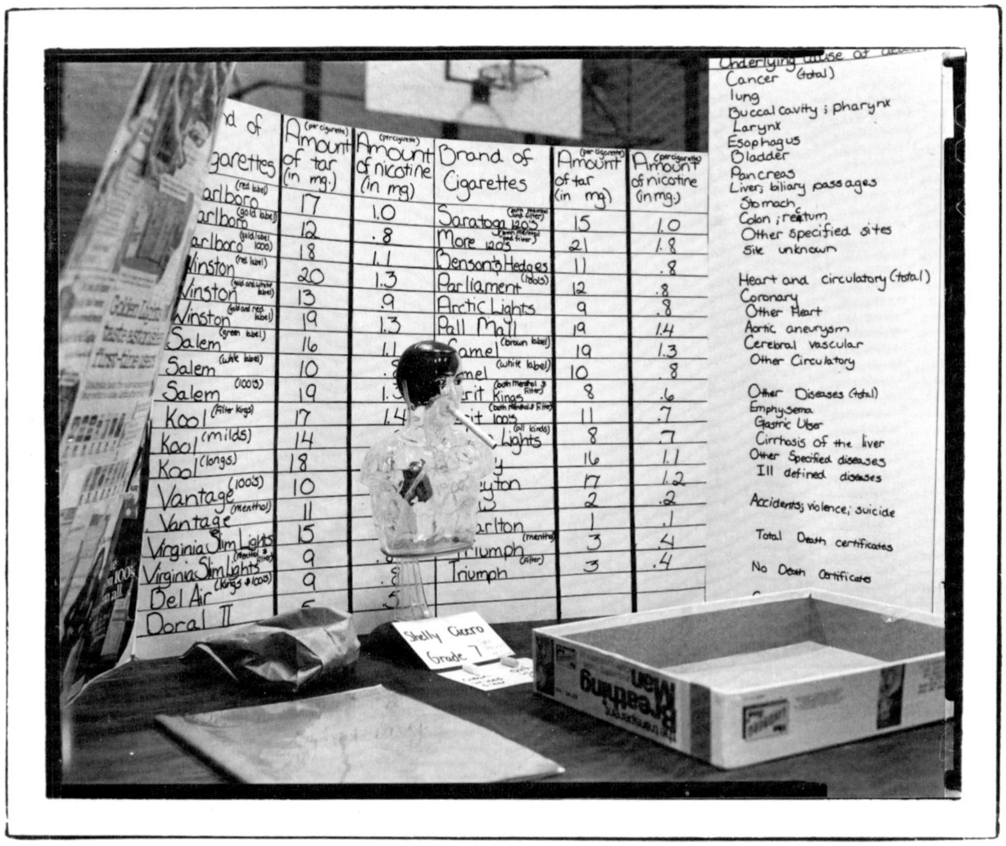

Junior High School Science Fair,
Suffield, Connecticut, 1980

Aluminum Cube on Glass Table,
Washington, D.C., 1980
Black-and-white photograph, gelatin
silver print, 8 x 10″ (20.3 x 25.3 cm)
Lent by the artist

Dental X-Rays, Suffield, Connecticut, 1980
Black-and-white photograph, gelatin
silver print, 8 x 10″ (20.3 x 25.3 cm)
Lent by the artist

Farm Machinery, Moscow, Idaho, 1980
Black-and-white photograph, gelatin
silver print, 8 x 10″ (20.3 x 25.3 cm)
Lent by the artist

Junior High School Science Fair, Suffield,
Connecticut, 1980
Black-and-white photograph, gelatin
silver print, 8 x 10″ (20.3 x 25.3 cm)
Lent by the artist

Snow Wheels Melting on the South Sides,
West Suffield, Connecticut, 1980
Black-and-white photograph, gelatin
silver print, 8 x 10″ (20.3 x 25.3 cm)
Lent by the artist

WPA Nutritional Puppets, Washington,
D.C., 1980
Black-and-white photograph, gelatin
silver print, 8 x 10″ (20.3 x 25.3 cm)
Lent by the artist

Peter D'Agostino

Quarks, 1980

Quarks, 1980
Video, color, 8 minutes
Lent by the artist

Video Program III
Wednesday, February 4–Sunday,
April 12, daily at 1:15 and 5:15

Willem de Kooning

Untitled I, 1980

Untitled III, 1978
Oil on canvas, 76⅝ x 87⅜″
(194.6 x 221.9 cm)
Xavier Fourcade, Inc., New York

Untitled IV, 1979
Oil on canvas, 80 x 70″
(203.2 x 177.8 cm)
Collection of Michael Rea

Untitled I, 1980
Oil on canvas, 80 x 70″
(203.2 x 177.8 cm)
Xavier Fourcade, Inc., New York

Richard Diebenkorn

Ocean Park #125, 1980

Ocean Park #107, 1978
Oil on canvas, 93 x 76″ (236.2 x 193 cm)
The Oakland Museum, Oakland, California

Ocean Park #125, 1980
Oil on canvas, 100 x 81″
(254 x 205.8 cm)
Whitney Museum of American Art, New York; Gift of an anonymous donor (by exchange), the Charles Simon Purchase Fund and purchase, Painting and Sculpture Committee 80.36

John Divola

Zuma #21, 1979

Zuma #18, 1979
Color photograph, Type C print,
14½ x 18″ (36.5 x 45.7 cm)
Lent by the artist, courtesy Robert
Freidus Gallery, New York

Zuma #21, 1979
Color photograph, Type C print,
14½ x 18″ (36.5 x 45.7 cm)
Lent by the artist, courtesy Robert
Freidus Gallery, New York

Zuma #38, 1979
Color photograph, Type C print,
14½ x 18″ (36.5 x 45.7 cm)
Collection of Howard Shapiro

Rackstraw Downes

The Tennis Courts in Riverside Park at 119th Street, 1978–80

The Tennis Courts in Riverside Park at 119th Street, 1978–80
Oil on canvas, 18¾ x 46¼″
(47.6 x117.5 cm)
Kornblee Gallery, New York

The Searsport Docks with the Unloading of the S.S. Inger, 1980
Oil on canvas, 15 x 53½″
(38.1 x 135.9 cm)
Odyssia Gallery, New York

Benni Efrat

Out and About, 1980

Out and About, 1980
Film installation, color
Lent by the artist

Rafael Ferrer

El Gran Canibal, 1979

El Gran Canibal, 1979
Acrylic on canvas, nylon, wood, 90 x 70 x 70″ (228.6 x 177.8 x 177.8 cm)
Hamilton Gallery of Contemporary Art, New York

Robert Fichter

The Cow, 1979

The Cow, 1979
Color photograph, Polaroid, 24 x 20″
(61 x 50.8 cm)
Lent by the artist, courtesy Robert
Freidus Gallery, New York

Lackland Air Force Base, 1979
Color photograph, Polaroid, 24 x 20″
(61 x 50.8 cm)
Lent by the artist, courtesy Robert
Freidus Gallery, New York

Winged Flying Dog, 1979
Color photograph, Polaroid, 20 x 24″
(50.8 x 61 cm)
Collection of Robert Freidus

Vernon Fisher

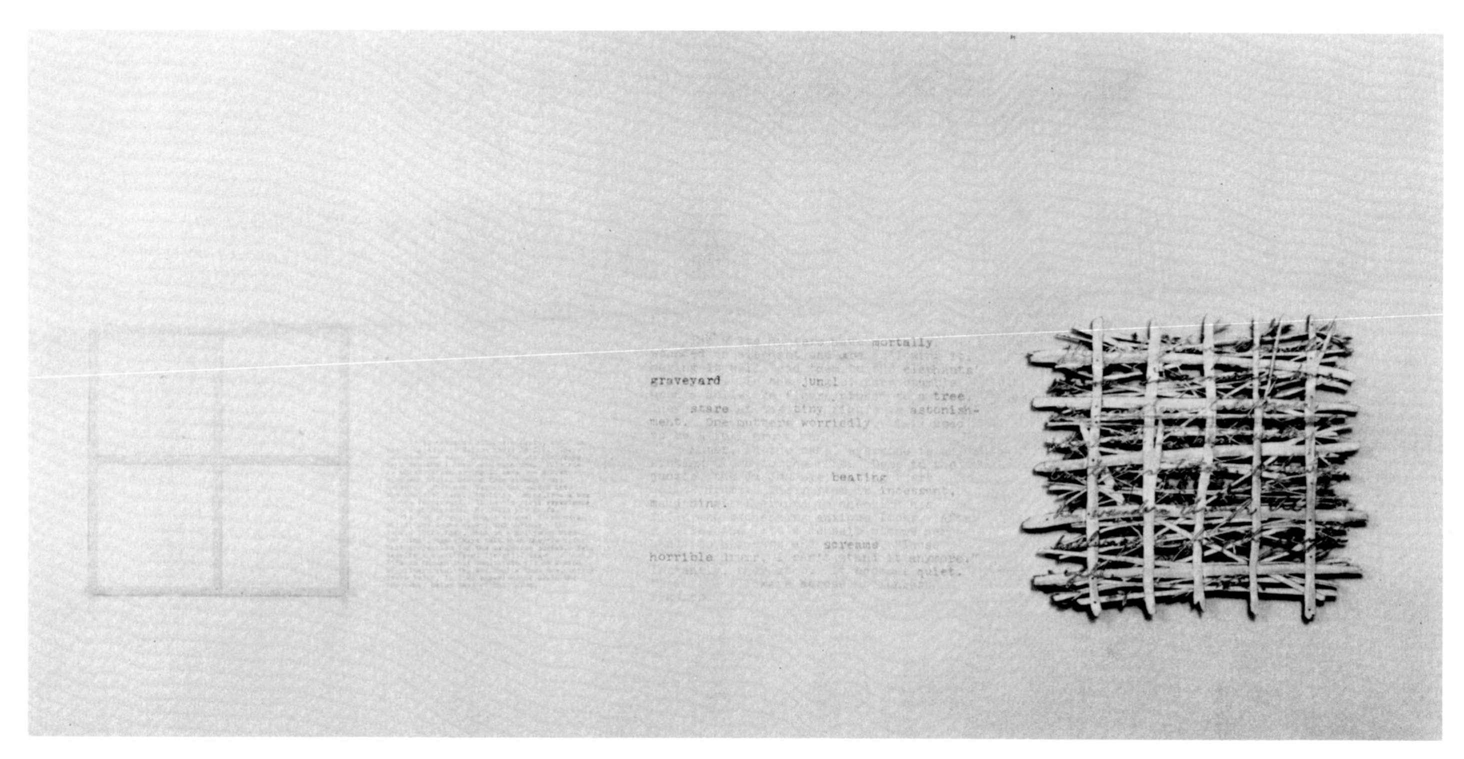

Tarzan's Adventure, 1980

Tarzan's Adventure, 1980
Acrylic on wood, and tape, graphite, watercolor and magic marker on wall; three units, 48 x 174″ (121.9 x 442 cm) overall
Lent by the artist, courtesy Delahunty Gallery, Dallas

Kit Fitzgerald and John Sanborn

Olympic Fragments, 1980

Olympic Fragments, 1980
Video, color, 10 minutes
Electronic Arts Intermix, New York

Video Program IV
Wednesday, February 4–Sunday, April 12, daily at 2:00, also Tuesdays at 6:15

Richard Fleischner

The Baltimore Project, 1978–80

Slide presentation of the following works:

The Baltimore Project, 1978–80
Granite and corten steel; ten elements,
2½ acres overall
Installation for Woodlawn, Maryland

Fence/Covered Fence, 1979–80
Wood, 14 x 113 x 300′
(4.2 x 33.9 x 90 m)
Installation for XIII Winter Olympic
Games, Lake Placid, New York

Hollis Frampton

Still from *Otherwise Unexplained Fires*, 1978
Film, color, 14 minutes
Collection of the artist

Gloria, 1979
Film, color, 10 minutes
Lent by the artist

Film Program I
Wednesday, February 4–Thursday, February 19, daily at 1:15; Tuesday, February 10, at 6:00

Richard Francisco

Constellation, 1980

Constellation, 1980
Enamel and acrylic on balsa wood,
63 x 164 x 1½" (160 x 416.6 x 3.8 cm)
Lent by the artist, courtesy Linda Farris Gallery, Seattle, Washington, and Betty Parsons Gallery, New York

Robert Frank

Still from *Life Dances On*, 1980

Life Dances On, 1980
Film, black and white, 30 minutes
Lent by the artist

Film Program III
Friday, February 20–Sunday, March 8, daily at 1:15; Tuesday, February 24, at 6:00

Howard Fried

Condom, 1979–80

Condom, 1979–80
Video, color, 35 minutes
Lent by the artist

Video Program II
Wednesday, February 4–Sunday,
April 12, daily at 12:30 and 4:30

Benno Friedman

New Forest, England, 1980

Deserted Building, Edinburgh, 1980
Black-and-white photograph, chemically altered silver print, and pencil on paper, 16 x 40″ (40.6 x 101.6 cm)
Lent by the artist, courtesy Photograph Gallery, New York

New Forest, England, 1980
Black-and-white photograph, chemically altered silver print, and pencil on paper, 20 x 16″ (50.8 x 40.6 cm)
Lent by the artist, courtesy Photograph Gallery, New York

Jedd Garet

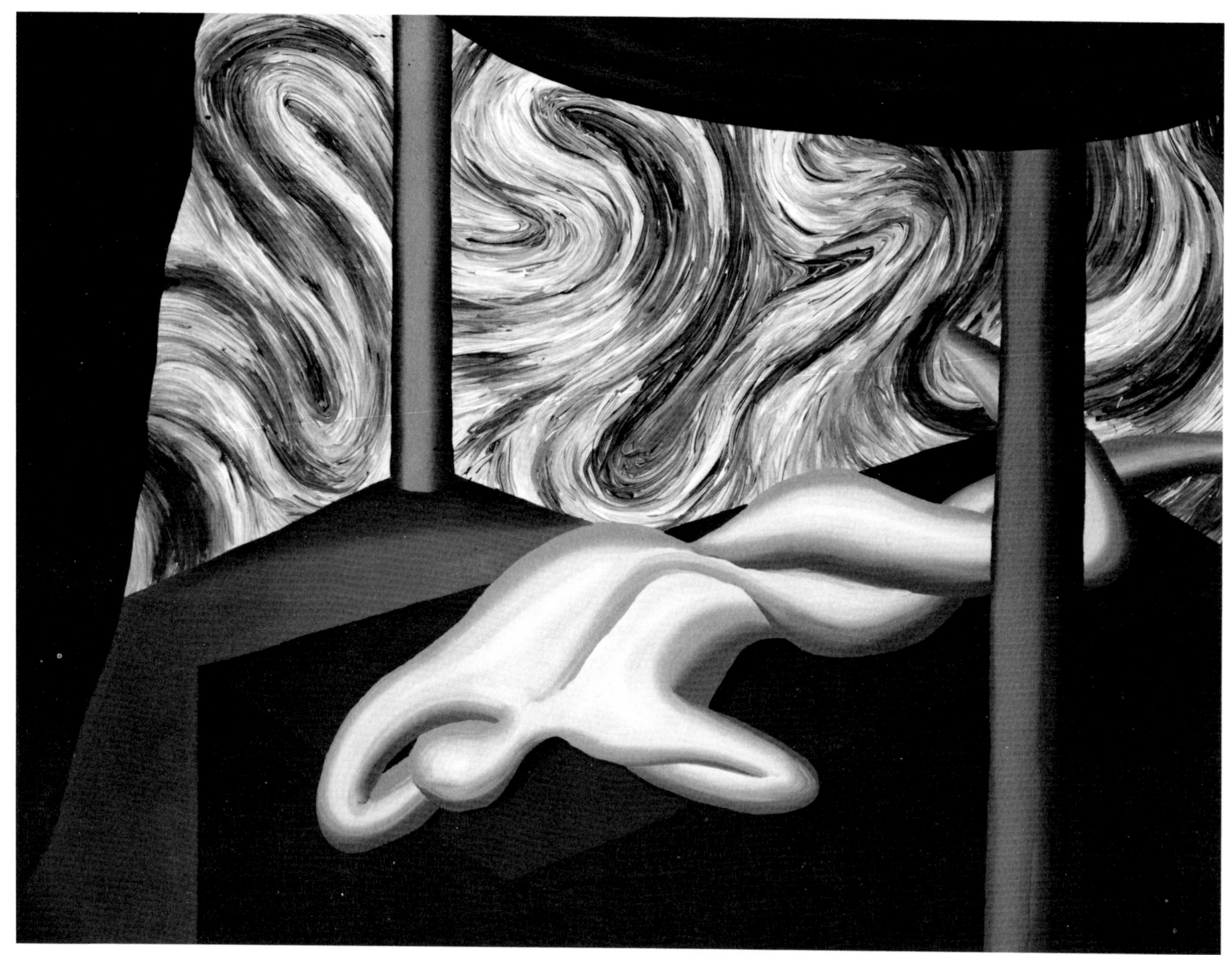

Yellow Fever, 1980

Flaming Colossus, 1980
Acrylic on canvas, 95½ x 69½″
(242.6 x 176.5 cm)
Private collection

Yellow Fever, 1980
Acrylic on canvas, 69½ x 95½″
(176.5 x 242.6 cm)
Robert Miller Gallery, New York

Ernie Gehr

Still from *Eureka,* 1979

Eureka, 1979
Film, black and white, 33 minutes
Filmmakers Cooperative, New York

Film Program I
Wednesday, February 4–Thursday, February 19, daily at 1:15; Tuesday, February 10, at 6:00

Barry Gerson

Still from *Exposed Fragrances*, 1980

Exposed Fragrances, 1980
Film, color, 8 minutes
The American Federation of Arts, New York

Hidden Tracings, 1980
Film, color, 3 minutes
The American Federation of Arts, New York

Film Program V
Tuesday, March 10–Thursday, March 26, daily at 1:15; Tuesday, March 10, and Tuesday, March 24, at 6:00

Davidson Gigliotti

After Montgolfier, 1979

After Montgolfier, 1979
Video, color, 10 minutes
Lent by the artist

Video Program I
Wednesday, February 4–Sunday, April 12, daily at 11:30 and 3:30

Frank Gillette

Aransas, Axis of Observation, 1979

Aransas, Axis of Observation, 1979
Video and photographic installation
University Art Museum, Berkeley,
California; Gift of James and
Ann Harithas

Bette Gordon

Still from *Empty Suitcases*, 1980

Empty Suitcases, 1980
Film, color, 53 minutes
Lent by the artist

Film Program VII
Friday, March 10–Sunday, April 12, daily
at 1:15; Tuesday, March 31, at 6:00

Shalom Gorewitz

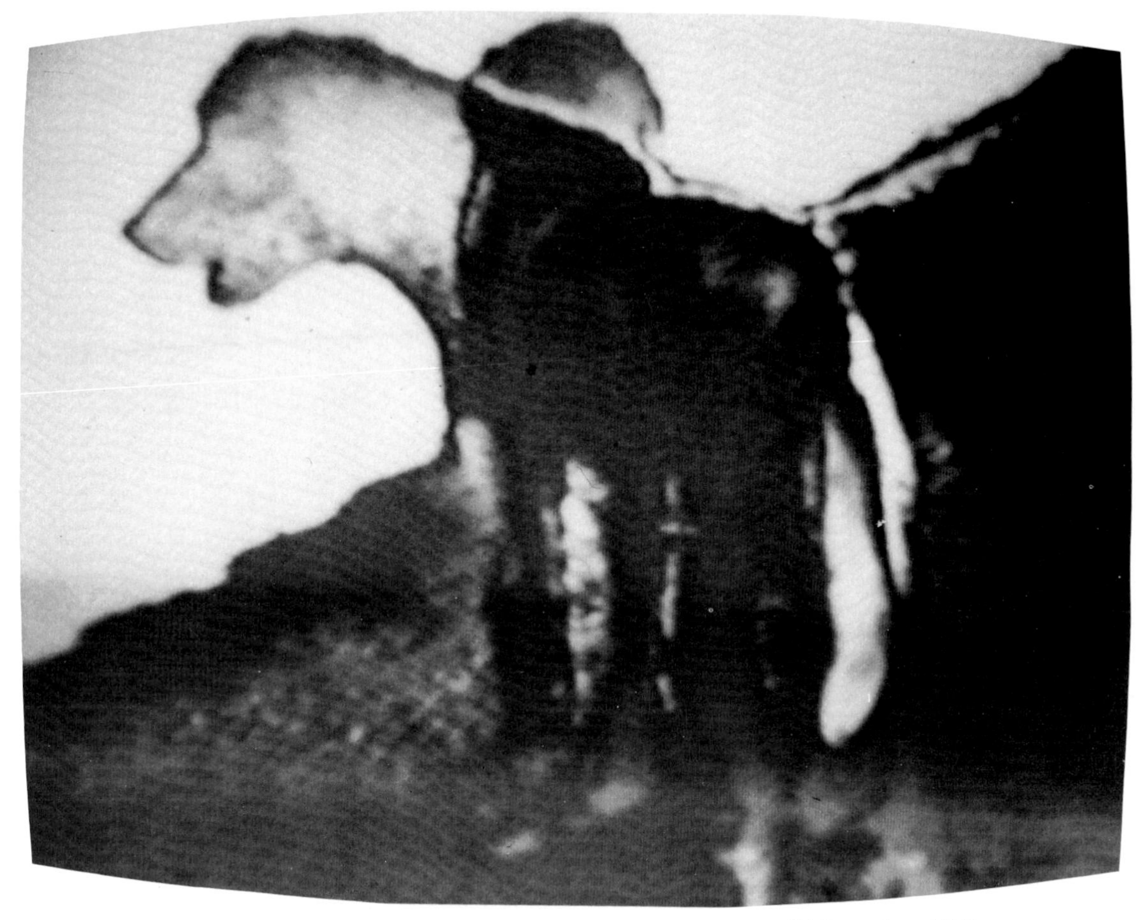

El Corandero, 1979

El Corandero, 1979
Video, color, 6 minutes
Lent by the artist

Delta Visions, 1980
Video, color, 5 minutes
Lent by the artist

Video Program I
Wednesday, February 4–Sunday,
April 12, daily at 11:30 and 3:30

Larry Gottheim

Still from *Tree of Knowledge: Elective Affinities, Part IV*, 1980

Tree of Knowledge: Elective Affinities, Part IV, 1980
Film, color, 65 minutes
Lent by the artist

Film Program VI
Tuesday, March 10–Thursday, March 26, daily at 3:15; Tuesday, March 17, at 6:00

Jan Groover

Untitled #275, 1980

Untitled #88, 1980
Black-and-white photograph, palladium platinum print, 10 x 8″
(25.4 x 20.3 cm)
Lent by the artist, courtesy Sonnabend Gallery, New York

Untitled #275, 1980
Black-and-white photograph, palladium platinum print, 10 x 8″
(25.4 x 20.3 cm)
Lent by the artist, courtesy Sonnabend Gallery, New York

Untitled #672, 1980
Black-and-white photograph, palladium platinum print, 10 x 8″
(25.4 x 20.3 cm)
Lent by the artist, courtesy Sonnabend Gallery, New York

Duane Hanson

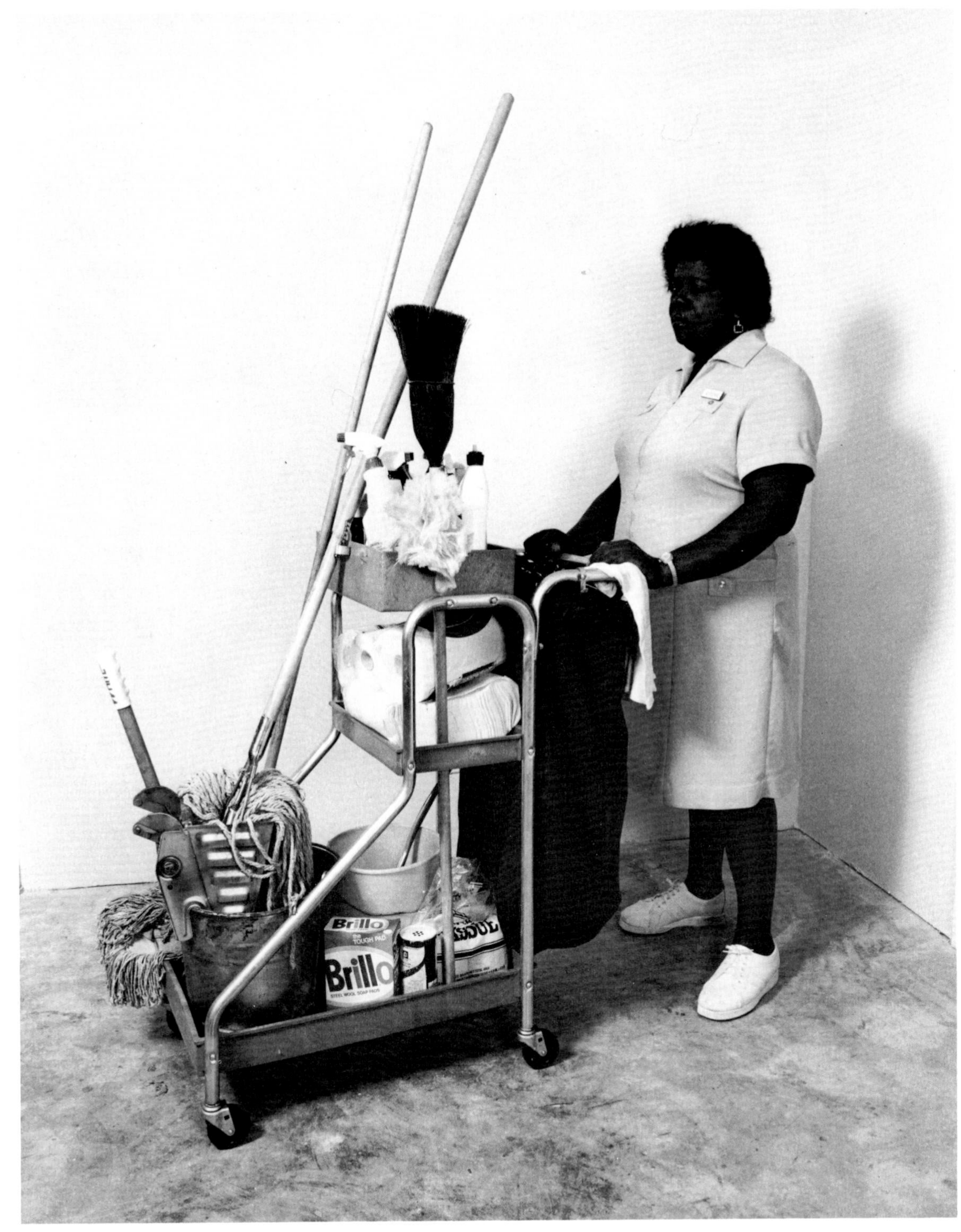

Cleaning Woman, 1980

Cleaning Woman, 1980
Polyvinyl polychromed in oil, life size
Collection of Martin Margulies

Martha Haslanger

Still from *Circus Riders,* 1979

Circus Riders, 1979
Film, color, 18 minutes
Lent by the artist

Film Program V
Tuesday, March 10–Thursday, March 26, daily at 1:15; Tuesday, March 10, and Tuesday, March 24, at 6:00

David Haxton

Shadows from Torn Magenta on White, 1980

Shadows from Torn Magenta on White, 1980
Color photograph, Type C print,
24 x 30" (61 x 76.2 cm)
Lent by the artist, courtesy Sonnabend Gallery, New York

Shadows from White with Holes, 1980
Color photograph, Type C print,
24 x 30" (61 x 76.2 cm)
Lent by the artist, courtesy Sonnabend Gallery, New York

Painting Room Lights, 1980
Film, color, 10 minutes
Lent by the artist
Film Program V
Tuesday, March 10–Thursday, March 26, daily at 1:15; Tuesday, March 10, and Tuesday, March 24, at 6:00

Al Held

M's Passage, 1980
Acrylic on canvas, 9½ x 16′
(2.8 x 4.8 m)
Collection of the artist, courtesy
André Emmerich Gallery, New York

Flow II, 1980–81
Acrylic on canvas, 9 x 18′
(2.7 x 5.4 m)
André Emmerich Gallery, New York

Nancy Holt

30 Below, 1979

Slide presentation of the following works:

Stone Enclosure: Rock Rings, 1977–78
Hand-quarried schist; height of ring walls 10′ (3 m), diameter of outer ring 40′ (12 m), diameter of inner ring 20′ (6 m), thickness of ring walls 2′ (.6 m)
Installation for Western Washington University, Bellingham, Washington
Mason: Al Poynter

30 Below, 1979
Brick with concrete, steel and concrete block foundation, 30′ (9 m) high, 9′ 4″ (2.8 m) diameter
Arches aligned with North Star
Installation for XIII Winter Olympic Games, Lake Placid, New York

Wild Spot, 1979–80
Wrought iron and native wild flowers; height of outer ring 10′ (3 m), diameter 10′ (3 m)
Installation for Wellesley College, Wellesley, Massachusetts

Bryan Hunt

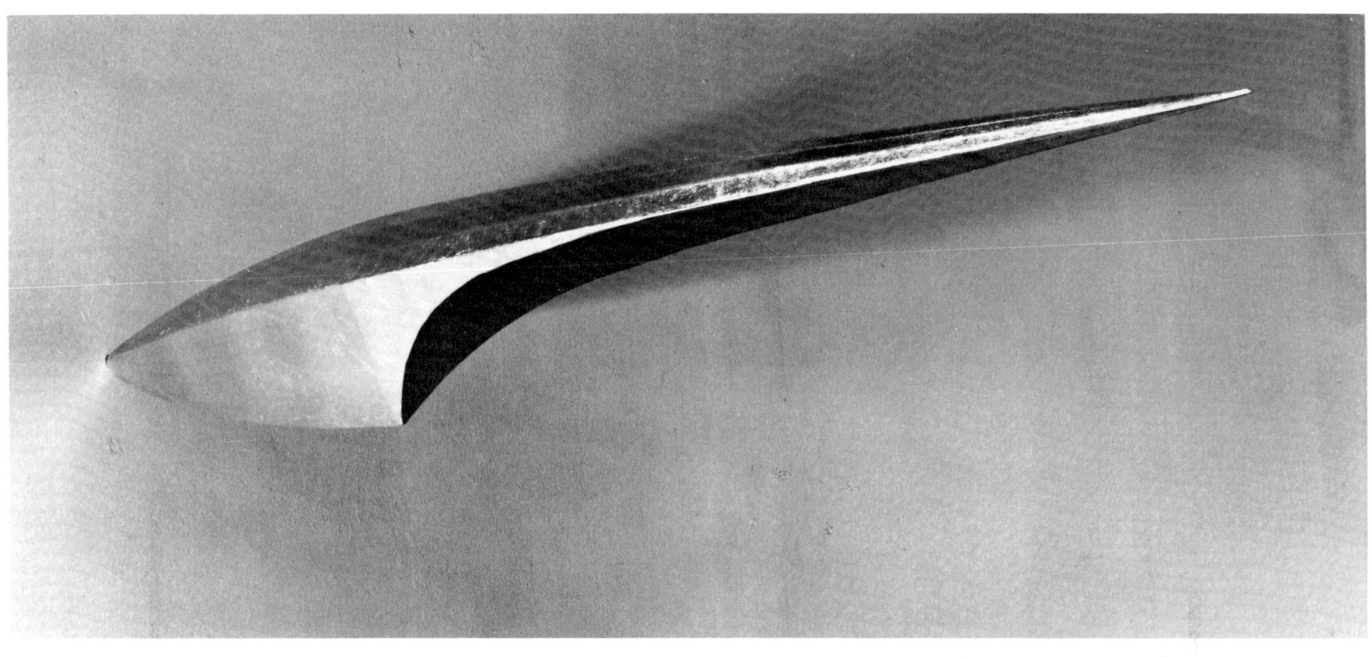

Nineteen Eighty-Six, 1980

Ancient Mariner, 1980
Wood and silk paper with gold leaf; 64″ (162.6 cm) long, 7″ (17.8 cm) diameter
Lent by the artist, courtesy Blum/Helman Gallery, New York

Nineteen Eighty-Six, 1980
Wood and silk paper with copper leaf; 65″ (165.1 cm) long, 9″ (23 cm) diameter
Lent by the artist, courtesy Blum/Helman Gallery, New York

Taka Iimura

Double Identities (On Turning the Double Negative to the Positive), 1979

Double Identities (On Turning the Double Negative to the Positive), 1979
Video, color, 8 minutes
Lent by the artist

Video Program III
Wednesday, February 4–Sunday, April 12, daily at 1:15 and 5:15

Ken Jacobs

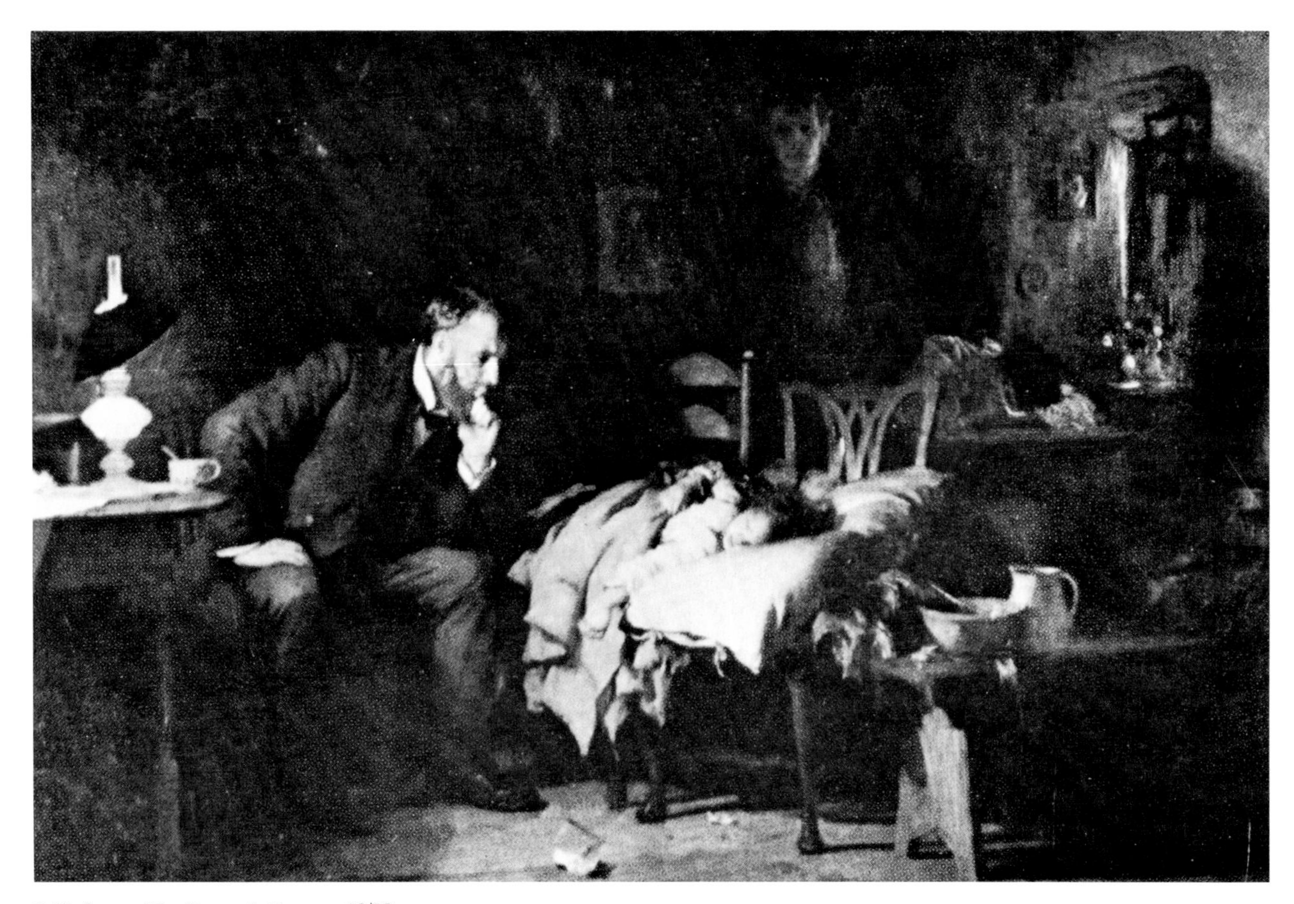

Still from *The Doctor's Dream*, 1979 (reproduction of the oil painting *The Doctor*, 1881, by Sir Luke Fildes; Tate Gallery, London)

The Doctor's Dream, 1979
Film, black and white, 26 minutes
Lent by the artist

Film Program I
Wednesday, February 4–Thursday, February 19, daily at 1:15; Tuesday, February 10, at 6:00

Neil Jenney

Window #6, 1976 and 1980

Meltdown Morning, 1972 and 1980
Oil on wood, 25½ x 113″
(84.8 x 287 cm) including frame
Lent by the artist

Window #6, 1976 and 1980
Oil on wood, 39 x 57¼″ (99 x 145.4 cm)
including frame
Lent by the artist

Bill Jensen

White Heat, 1978–79

Ryder's Eye, 1978–79
Oil on linen, 20 x 16" (50.8 x 40.6 cm)
Collection of Reeds Foundation, Boston

White Heat, 1978–79
Oil on linen, 22 x 16" (55.2 x 40.6 cm)
Private collection

Steve Keister

U.S.O. #58, 1980

Untitled, 1980
Industrial carpeting, fluorescent
Plexiglas and acrylic on wood,
50 x 54 x 56″ (127 x 137.2 x 142.3 cm)
Lent by the artist, courtesy Blum/
Helman Gallery, New York

U.S.O. #58, 1980
Formica and acrylic on wood,
15 x 27 x 21″ (38.1 x 68.6 x 53.3 cm)
Private collection

U.S.O. #63, 1980
Feathers, mirrored Plexiglas and acrylic
on wood, 21 x 28 x 30″
(53.3 x 71.1 x 76.2 cm)
Collection of Carl and Katherine Lobel

Ellsworth Kelly

Untitled, 1979

Untitled, 1979
Birchwood, 75 x 170 x 1″
(190.5 x 431.8 x 2.5 cm)
Lent by the artist, courtesy Blum/
Helman Gallery, New York, and Leo
Castelli Gallery, New York

Edward Kienholz

Sollie 17 (detail), 1979–80

Sollie 17, 1979–80
Mixed media environment,
10 x 28 x 14′ (3 x 8.4 x 4.2 m)
Galerie Maeght, New York

Robert Kushner

Happy Hour, 1980

Same Outfit, 1979
Acrylic on cotton with appliqué; two panels, 122 x 42″ (310 x 106.7 cm) each, 122 x 97″ (310 x 246.4 cm) overall
Lent by the artist, courtesy Holly Solomon Gallery, New York

Happy Hour, 1980
Acrylic on cotton, 67 x 188″ (170.2 x 477.6 cm)
Collection of Holly and Horace Solomon

George Landow

Still from *On the Marriage Broker Joke as Cited by Sigmund Freud in Wit and Its Relation to the Unconscious or Can the Avant-garde Artist be Wholed?* 1978–81

On the Marriage Broker Joke as Cited by Sigmund Freud in Wit and Its Relation to the Unconscious or Can the Avant-garde Artist be Wholed? 1978–81
Film, color, 20 minutes
Filmmakers Cooperative, New York

Film Program III
Friday, February 20–Sunday, March 8, daily at 1:15; Tuesday, February 24, at 6:00

William Larson

Untitled, 1980

Untitled, 1979
Color photograph, Type C print,
14½ x 14⅛" (36.5 x 36 cm)
Lent by the artist, courtesy
Light Gallery, New York

Untitled, 1979
Color photograph, Type C print,
14½ x 14⅛" (36.5 x 36 cm)
Lent by the artist, courtesy
Light Gallery, New York

Untitled, 1980
Color photograph, dye-transfer print,
13½ x 13¼" (34.3 x 33.7 cm)
Lent by the artist, courtesy
Light Gallery, New York

Peter Lodato

Near Opposites, 1980
Sheet rock, gloss and flat enamel on wall; two rectangles, 132 x 108″ (335.3 x 274.3 cm) each
Lent by the artist, courtesy Rosamund Felsen Gallery, Los Angeles, and Livet Reichard Company, Inc., New York and Fort Worth, Texas

Black and White #4, 1980
Sheet rock, gloss and flat enamel on wall; two rectangles, 132 x 108″ (335.3 x 274.3 cm) each
Installation at Rosamund Felsen Gallery, Los Angeles, January–February, 1980

Kim MacConnel

Greek, 1980

Greek, 1980
Acrylic on cotton, 98 x 128″
(248.9 x 315 cm)
Lent by the artist, courtesy
Holly Solomon Gallery, New York

Sharkey, 1980
Acrylic on cotton, 101 x 109″
(256.5 x 276.9 cm)
Lent by the artist, courtesy
Holly Solomon Gallery, New York

Robert Mapplethorpe

Lee Leigh, 1980 © Robert Mapplethorpe

Auto Portrait (in Drag), 1980
Black-and-white photograph, silver print, 20 x 16″ (50.8 x 40.6 cm)
Robert Miller Gallery, New York

Flower Arrangement, New York City, 1980
Black-and-white photograph, silver print, 20 x 16″ (50.8 x 40.6 cm)
Robert Miller Gallery, New York

Lee Leigh, 1980
Black-and-white photograph, silver print, 20 x 16″ (50.8 x 40.6 cm)
Robert Miller Gallery, New York

Joel Meyerowitz

Florida Pool at Dusk, 1979

Cape Cod, Provincetown (Fence at Dusk), 1979
Color photograph, Type C print,
16 x 20″ (40.6 x 50.8 cm)
Lent by the artist

Florida Pool at Dusk, 1979
Color photograph, Type C print,
20 x 16″ (50.8 x 40.6 cm)
Lent by the artist

St. Louis and the Arch (Runner in Fountain), 1979
Color photograph, Type C print,
16 x 20″ (40.6 x 50.8 cm)
Lent by the artist

Duane Michals

Portrait of Richard Whelan and a White Cup, 1980

Knives, 1980
Ink on paper, and black-and-white photograph, 6 x 8″
(15.2 x 20.3 cm) each
Sidney Janis Gallery, New York

Nude Study of S.C., 1980
Ink on paper, and black-and-white photograph, 6 x 8″
(15.2 x 20.3 cm) each
Sidney Janis Gallery, New York

Portrait of Richard Whelan and a White Cup, 1980
Oil on black-and-white photograph, 11 x 14″ (27.9 x 35.6 cm)
Sidney Janis Gallery, New York

Richard Misrach

Sounion, Greece II, 1979 © Richard Misrach

Los Angeles I, 1979
Color photograph, Type C print,
30 x 40″ (76.2 x 101.6 cm)
Grapestake Gallery, San Francisco

Sounion, Greece II, 1979
Color photograph, Type C print,
30 x 40″ (76.2 x 101.6 cm)
Grapestake Gallery, San Francisco

Mary Miss

Veiled Landscape, 1979–80

Slide presentation of the following works:

Staged Gates, 1979
Wood, 12½ x 50 x 120′
(3.75 x 15 x 36 m) overall
Installation for Dayton, Ohio

Veiled Landscape, 1979–80
Wood, metal and wire screen, 400′
(120 m) long
Installation for XIII Winter Olympic
Games, Lake Placid, New York

Owen Morrel

Omega, 1980

Slide presentation of the following works:

Asylum, 1978–79
Steel and plastic mirror, 35 x 40 x 30′
(10.5 x 12 x 9 m) overall
Installation for American Thread
Building rooftop, New York

Omega, 1980
Steel and plastic mirror, 44 x 42 x 110′
(13.2 x 12.6 x 33 m) overall
Installation for Artpark, Lewiston,
New York

Robert Moskowitz

Big Picture, 1979–80

Big Picture, 1979–80
Oil on canvas; three panels, 96 x 64¼″
(243.8 x 163.8 cm) each, 96 x 228¾″
(243.8 x 592.5 cm) overall
Lent by the artist

Grant Mudford

Los Angeles, 1979

Hollywood, 1978
Black-and-white photograph, gelatin silver print, 24 x 20″ (61 x 50.8 cm)
Lent by the artist, courtesy Rosamund Felsen Gallery, Los Angeles

Under Ocean Boulevard, 1979–80
Black-and-white photograph, gelatin silver print, 23⅛ x 18¾″ (58 x 47 cm)
Lent by the artist, courtesy Rosamund Felsen Gallery, Los Angeles

Los Angeles, 1979
Black-and-white photograph, gelatin silver print, 24 x 20″ (61 x 50.8 cm)
Lent by the artist, courtesy Rosamund Felsen Gallery, Los Angeles

Elizabeth Murray

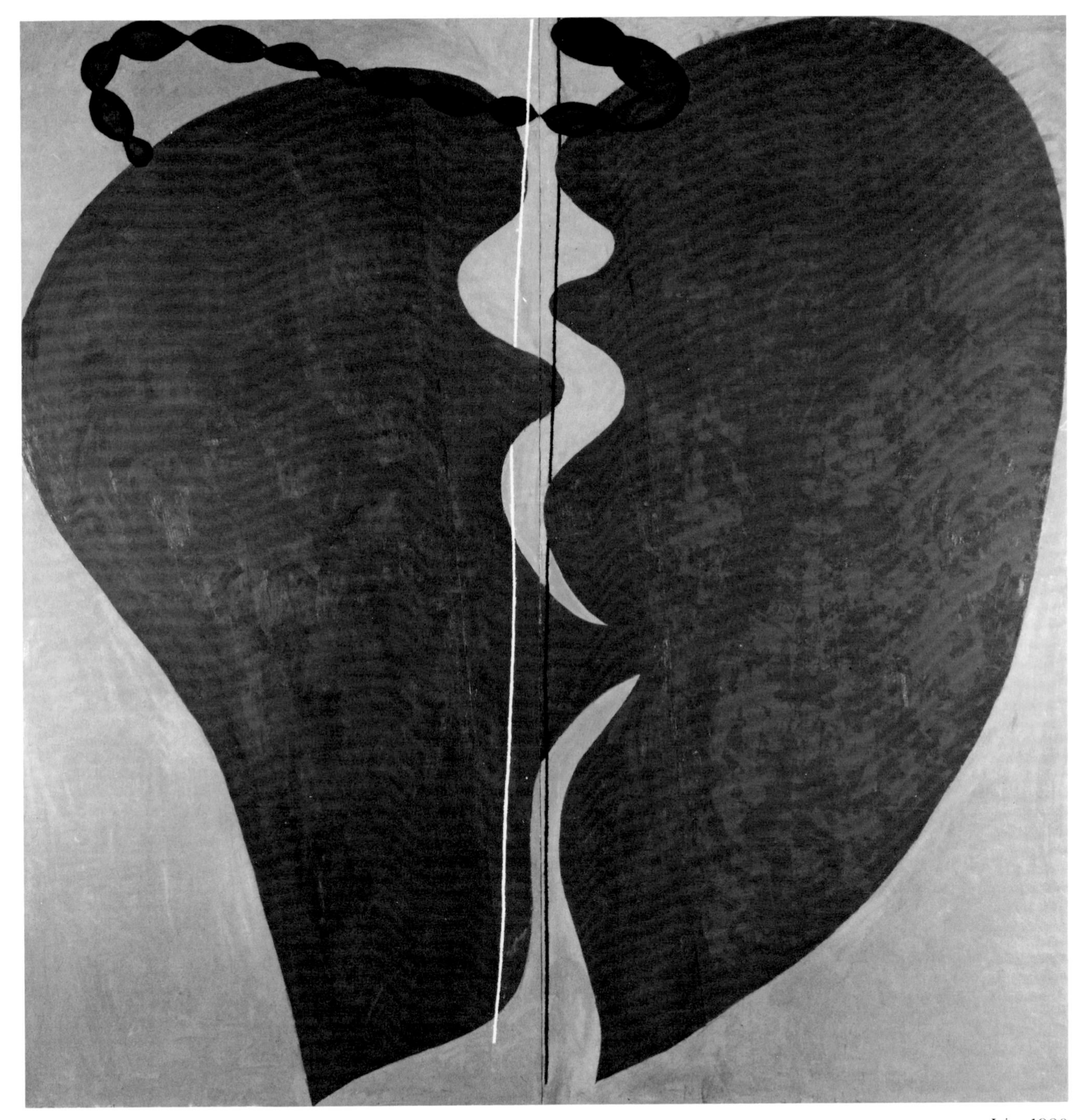

Join, 1980

Writer, 1979
Oil on canvas, 137 x 74″ (348 x 188 cm)
The St. Louis Art Museum; Purchase, funds given by Mrs. Theodore R. Gamble and the Contemporary Art Society

Join, 1980
Oil on canvas, 133 x 120″
(337.8 x 304.8 cm)
Paula Cooper Gallery, New York

Andrew Noren

Still from *Charmed Particles,* 1979

Charmed Particles, 1979
Film, black and white, 78 minutes
Filmmakers Cooperative, New York

Film Program VIII
Friday, March 27–Sunday, April 12,
daily at 3:15; Tuesday, April 7, at 6:00

Arthur Ollman

Albany and Cactus, 1979 © Arthur Ollman

Albany and Cactus, 1979
Color photograph, Type C print,
16 x 20″ (40.6 x 50.8 cm)
Grapestake Gallery, San Francisco

Place Dauphine, 1979
Color photograph, Type C print,
16 x 20″ (40.6 x 50.8 cm)
Grapestake Gallery, San Francisco

Calvi, Corsica, 1980
Color photograph, Type C print,
16 x 20″ (40.6 x 50.8 cm)
Grapestake Gallery, San Francisco

Dennis Oppenheim

A Station for Detaining and Blinding Radio-Active Horses, 1980

Slide presentation of the following works:

An Operation for Mining, Elevating and Converting Underground Memories of a Fifth Season. An Around the Clock Activity, 1980
Steel and wood, motorized,
24 x 18 x 80′ (30 x 5.4 x 24 m)
Installation for Cranbrook Academy of Art, Detroit

A Station for Detaining and Blinding Radio-Active Horses, 1980
Concrete, steel, canvas, mixed media, motorized, 24 x 100 x 650′
(7.2 x 30 x 195 m)
Installation for Wenkenpark, Basel, Switzerland

Nam June Paik

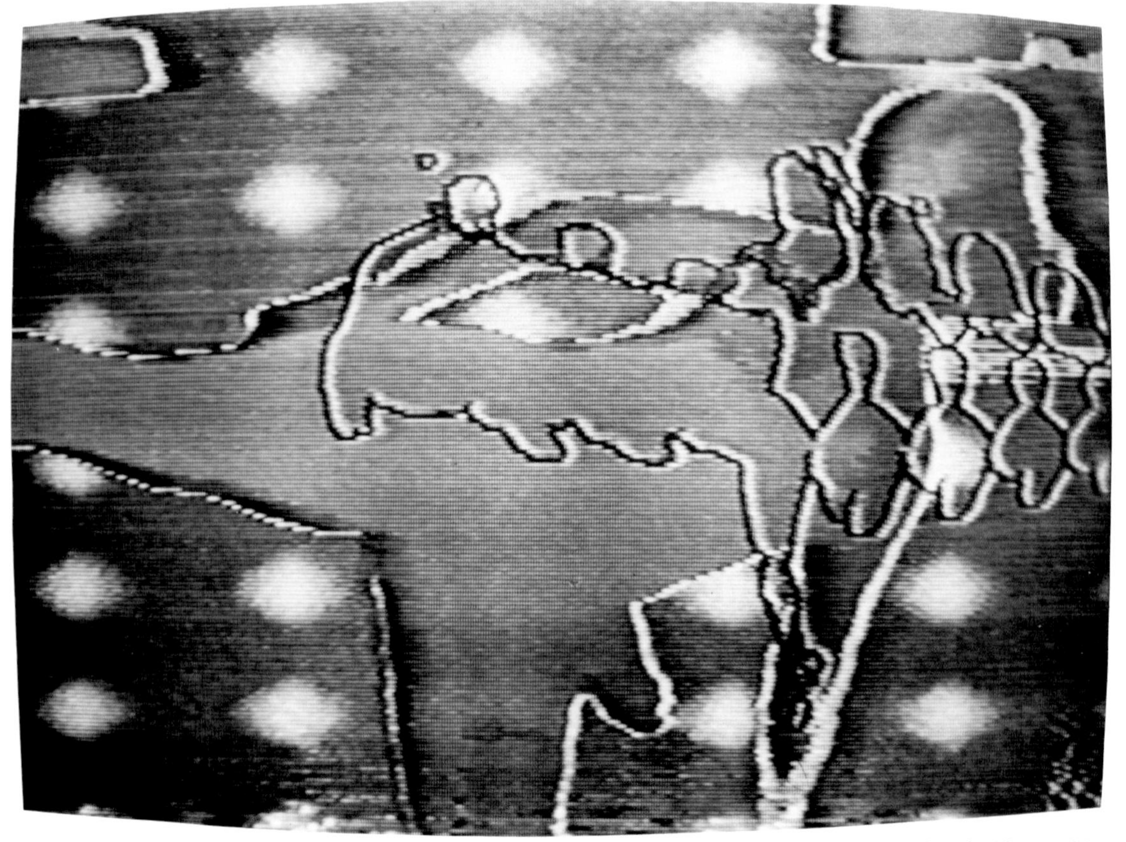

Lake Placid 80, 1980

Lake Placid 80, 1980
Video, color, 4 minutes
Electronic Arts Intermix, New York

Video Program IV
Wednesday, February 4–Sunday, April 12, daily at 2:00, Tuesdays at 6:15

Ed Paschke

Violencia, 1980

Brand Ex, 1980
Oil on canvas, 32 x 72″
(81.3 x 182.9 cm)
Lent by the artist, courtesy Phyllis Kind Gallery, New York and Chicago

Violencia, 1980
Oil on canvas, 74 x 96½″
(188 x 245.1 cm)
Lent by the artist, courtesy Phyllis Kind Gallery, New York and Chicago

Judy Pfaff

Deepwater, 1980
Mixed media installation at
Holly Solomon Gallery, New York,
September, 1980

Dragon, 1981
Mixed media installation
Lent by the artist, courtesy Holly
Solomon Gallery, New York

Katherine Porter

Truth Rescued from Romance, 1980

To Victor Jara, 1980
Oil on canvas, 87¼ x 103¾″
(221.6 x 363.5 cm)
David McKee Gallery, New York

Truth Rescued from Romance, 1980
Oil on canvas, 88½ x 86¼″
(224.8 x 219 cm)
David McKee Gallery, New York

Kenneth Price

Avocado and Wine, 1980

Avocado and Wine, 1980
Glazed ceramic, 6⅝ x 11⅜ x 5⅜″
(16.7 x 28.7 x 13.5 cm)
Private collection

Flag, 1980
Glazed ceramic, 9⅜ x 6¾ x 2⅝″
(23.6 x 17.1 x 6.6 cm)
Collection of Dorothy and Roy Lichtenstein

Orange Box, 1980
Glazed ceramic, 5¼ x 9⅛ x 8″
(13.3 x 23 x 20.3 cm)
Private collection

Martin Puryear

Bower, 1980

Na, 1979
Polychromed pine, 65″ (165.1 cm) diameter
Collection of Harry Lunn

Noatak, 1979
Polychromed pine, 74″ (188 cm) diameter
Collection of Chris Middendorf

Bower, 1980
Sitka spruce and pine, 64 x 97 x 28″ (162.6 x 246.4 x 71.1 cm)
Collection of Paul and Camille Oliver-Hoffman, courtesy Young/Hoffman Gallery, Chicago

Yvonne Rainer

Still from *Journeys from Berlin/1971*, 1980

Journeys from Berlin/1971, 1980
Film, color, 125 minutes
Lent by the artist

Film Program II
Wednesday, February 4–Thursday, February 19, daily at 3:15; Tuesday, February 17, at 5:45

Leland Rice

Wall Site (Spray Painted Lattice Against Wall), 1979

Wall Site (Blue Door), 1978–79
Color photograph, dye-coupler print,
37 x 29⅜″ (94 x 74 cm)
Lent by the artist, courtesy Rosamund Felsen Gallery, Los Angeles

Wall Site (P.S.1 Papered Wall), 1978–79
Color photograph, dye-coupler print,
29½ x 37″ (75 x 94 cm)
Lent by the artist, courtesy Rosamund Felsen Gallery, Los Angeles

Wall Site (Spray Painted Lattice Against Wall), 1979
Color photograph, dye-coupler print,
38 x 29½″ (97 x 75 cm)
Lent by the artist, courtesy Rosamund Felsen Gallery, Los Angeles

Bruce Robbins

Beyondo, 1980

Beyondo, 1980
Polymer paint and sand on wood and canvas, 84 x 126″ (213.4 x 320 cm)
Private collection

Vanquisher, 1980
Polymer paint and sand on wood and canvas, 90 x 80″ (228.6 x 203.2 cm)
Lent by the artist, courtesy Blum/Helman Gallery, New York

James Rosenquist

Untitled, 1980

Dog Descending a Staircase, 1979
Oil on canvas; three panels, 84 x 108″
(213.4 x 274.3 cm) overall
Private collection

Untitled, 1980
Oil on canvas, 78 x 66″
(198.1 x 167.6 cm)
Collection of Philip Johnson

Julian Schnabel

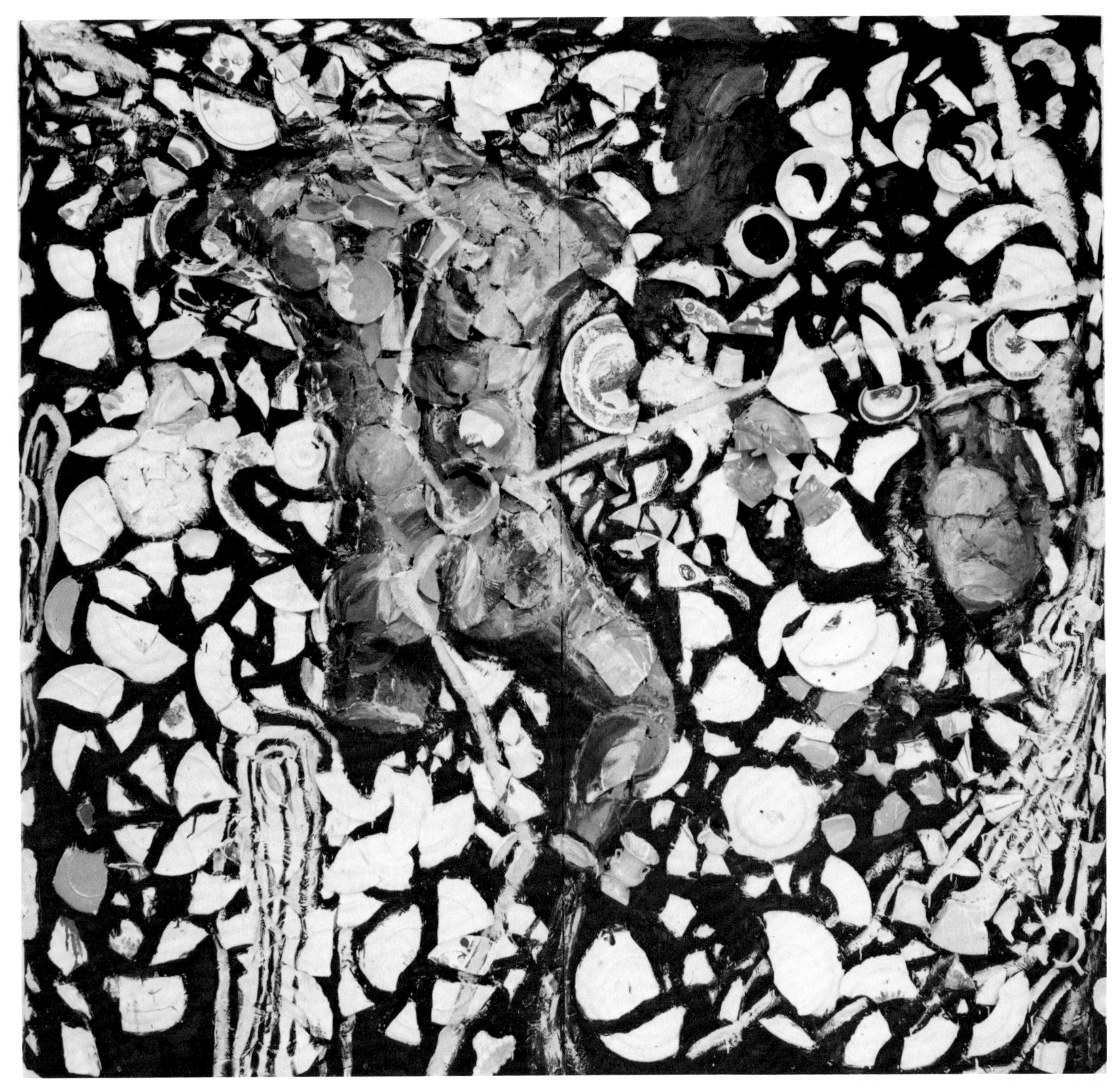

What To Do With a Corner in Madrid, 1980

Foufi Nouti in Hell, 1980
Oil on silk, 90 x 84″ (228.6 x 213.4 cm)
Mary Boone Gallery, New York

What To Do With a Corner in Madrid,
1980
Oil, plates, and putty on wood, 90 x 96″
(228.6 x 243.8 cm)
Collection of Barbara Jakobson

Victor Schrager

Untitled, 1979

Untitled, 1979
Color photograph, Polaroid, 24 x 20″
(61 x 50.8 cm)
Lent by the artist, courtesy Robert
Freidus Gallery, New York

Untitled, 1979
Color photograph, Polaroid, 24 x 20″
(61 x 50.8 cm)
Collection of Robert Freidus

Buky Schwartz

In Real Time, 1980

In Real Time, 1980
Video installation, two color cameras, four monitors, mirror and painted sections of walls
Created for this exhibition

Richard Serra

St. John's Rotary Arc, 1980

Slide presentation of the following works:

St. John's Rotary Arc, 1980
Corten steel, 12′ x 200′ x 2½″
(3.6 m x 60 m x 6.3 cm)
Installation at Rotary of the Holland Tunnel exit, New York

T.W.U., 1980
Corten steel; three plates,
36′ x 12′ x 2¾″
(10.7 m x 3.6 m x 6.5 cm) each
Installation at the intersection of Franklin Street and West Broadway, New York

Joel Shapiro

Untitled, 1980
Wood, 52⅞ x 64 x 45½″
(133.9 x 162.6 x 115.6 cm)
Paula Cooper Gallery, New York

Untitled, 1980
Bronze, 52⅞ x 64 x 45½″
(133.9 x 162.6 x 115.6 cm)
Lent by the artist, courtesy Paula
Cooper Gallery, New York

Untitled, 1980
Bronze, 8$\frac{5}{16}$ x 13½ x 6½″
(21.1 x 34.3 x 16.5 cm)
Lent by the artist, courtesy Paula
Cooper Gallery, New York

Sally Shapiro

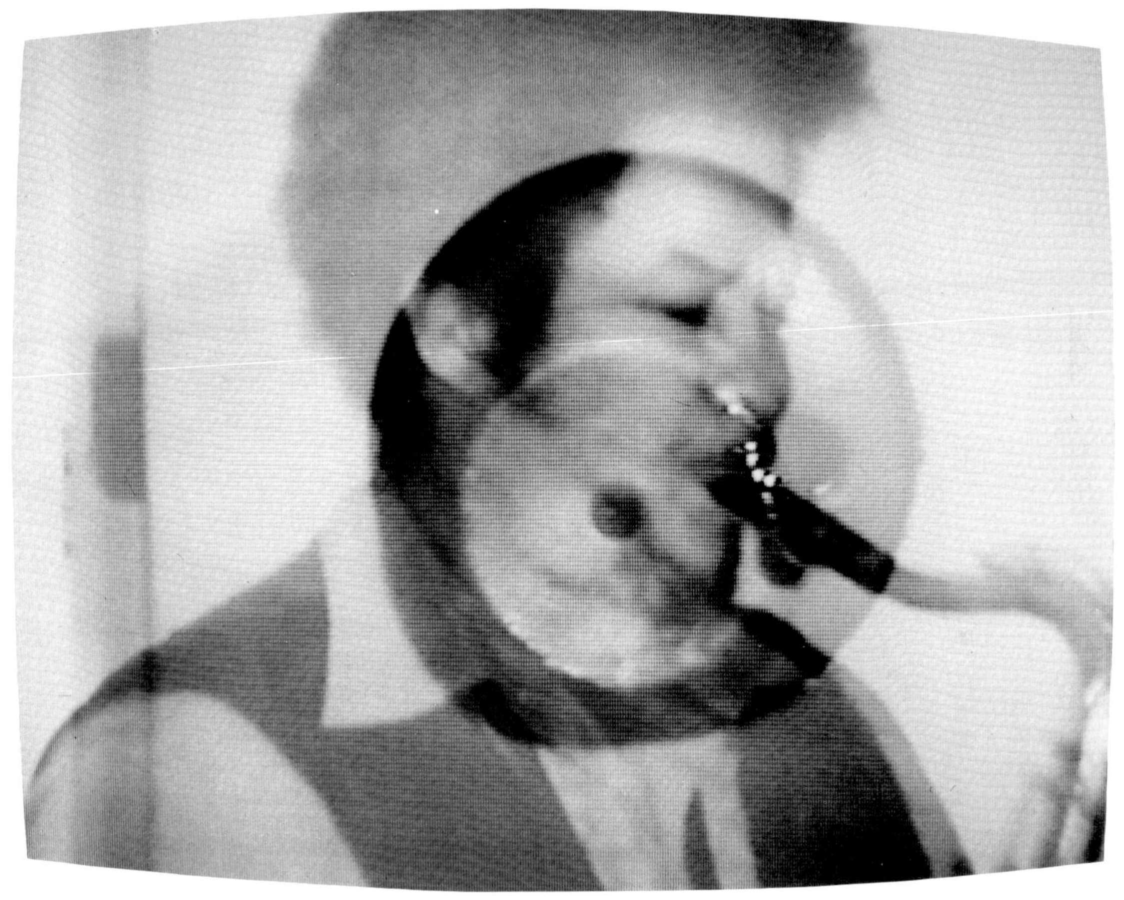

Transnotations, 1980

Transnotations, 1980
Video, color, 8 minutes
Lent by the artist

Video Program IV
Wednesday, February 4–Sunday,
April 12, daily at 2:00, Tuesdays at 6:15

Paul Sharits

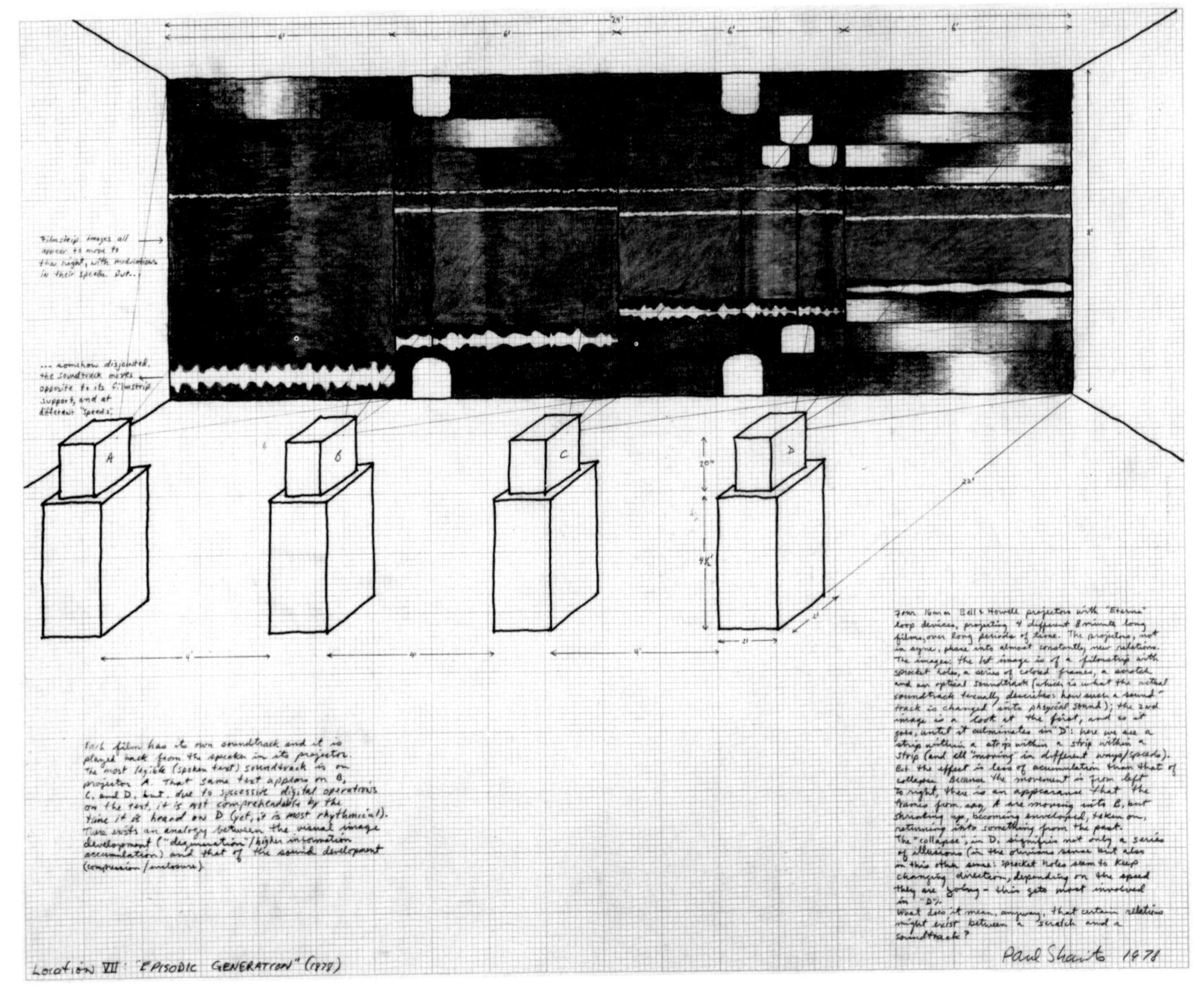

Drawing for *Episodic Generation*, 1978

Episodic Generation, 1979
Film installation, color, sound
Lent by the artist

Drawing for *Episodic Generation*, 1978
Pencil and ink on paper, 16 x 20″
(40.6 x 50.8 cm)
Collection of the artist

Richard Shaw

Mike Goes Back to T., 1980

Back to Stinson, 1980
Glazed porcelain with overglaze transfers, 37⅛ x 12 x 24″
(92.8 x 30.5 x 61 cm)
Braunstein Gallery, San Francisco, and Allan Frumkin Gallery, New York

House of Pencils with Two Volumes, 1980
Glazed porcelain with overglaze transfers, 8¾ x 9½ x 12″
(21.9 x 23.8 x 30 cm)
Braunstein Gallery, San Francisco, and Allan Frumkin Gallery, New York

Mike Goes Back to T., 1980
Glazed porcelain with overglaze transfers, 41¾ x 14 x 19″
(104.4 x 35.6 x 47.3 cm)
Braunstein Gallery, San Francisco, and Allan Frumkin Gallery, New York

Judith Shea

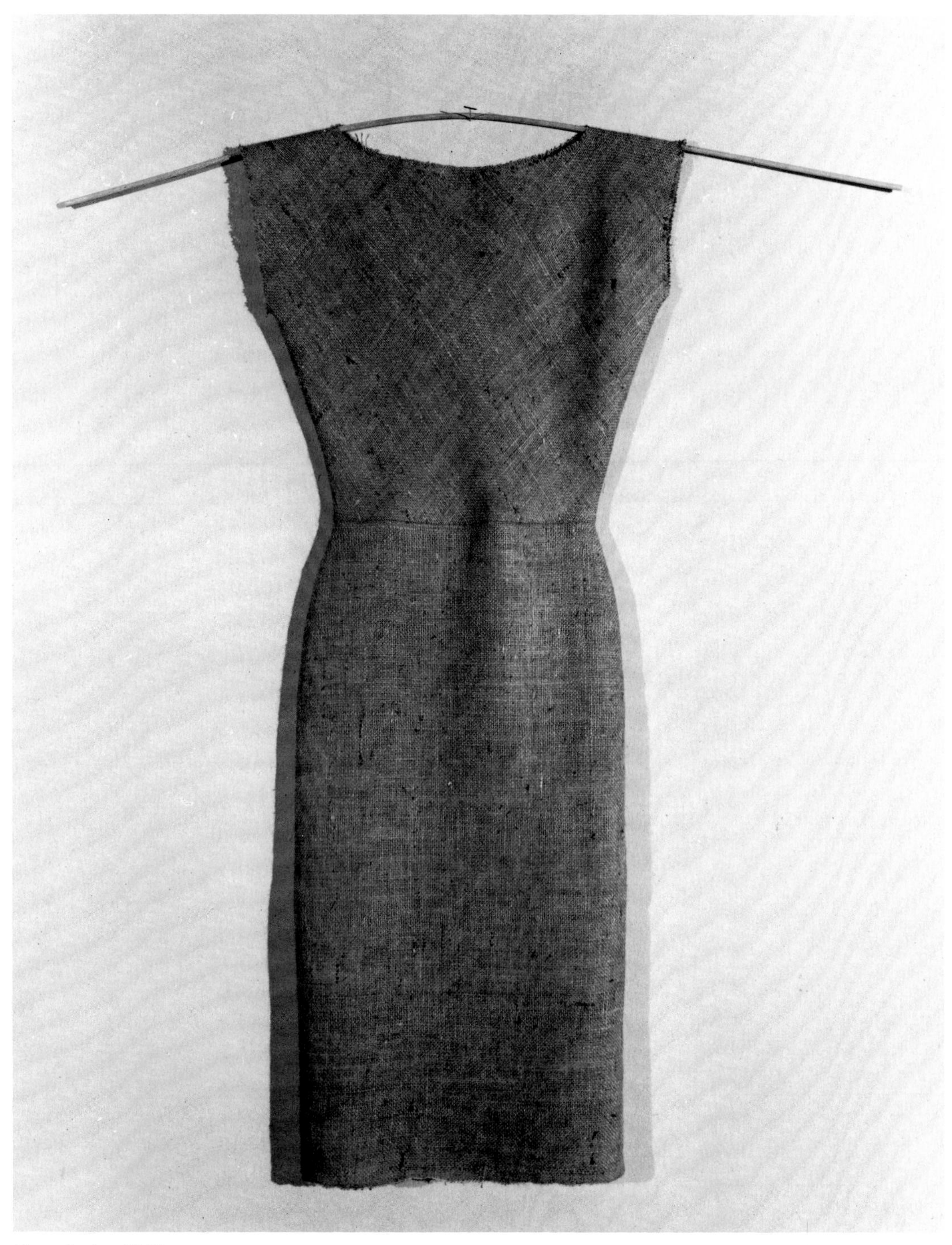

Exec. Sec'y., 1980

Exec. Sec'y, 1980
Burlap, 47½ x 48 x 3″
(119.3 x 121.9 x 7.6 cm)
Lent by the artist, courtesy Willard Gallery, New York

I Like Ike, 1980
Cotton canvas, 44 x 19 x 2″
(111.8 x 48.3 x 5.1 cm)
Lent by the artist, courtesy Willard Gallery, New York

Inaugural Ball, 1980
Cotton organdy, 67 x 24 x 1½″
(162.6 x 61 x 3.8 cm)
Lent by the artist, courtesy Willard Gallery, New York

Stuart Sherman

Still from *(Rock/String)*, 1979–80

6 Films (Fountain/Car, Baseball/TV, Flying, Hand/Water, Rock/String, Roller Coaster/ Reading), 1979–80
Film, black and white, 13 minutes
Lent by the artist

Film Program III
Friday, February 20–Sunday, March 8, daily at 1:15; Tuesday, February 24, at 6:00

Hollis Sigler

It Was All Play, 1980

It Was All Play, 1980
Oil on canvas, 42 x 60″
(106.7 x 152.4 cm)
Private collection, courtesy Barbara
Gladstone Gallery, New York

She Still Merengues, 1980
Oil on canvas, 42 x 60″
(106.7 x 152.4 cm)
Nancy Lurie Gallery, Chicago

Sandy Skoglund

Radioactive Cats, 1980

Radioactive Cats, 1980
Color photograph, Cibachrome print,
30 x 40″ (76.2 x 101.6 cm)
Collection of Marvin Heiferman

Revenge of the Goldfish, 1980
Color photograph, Cibachrome print,
30 x 40″ (76.2 x 101.6 cm)
Castelli Photographs, New York

Alexis Smith

Golden State, 1980

Golden State, 1980
Mixed media collage with found objects and paint on wall; three panels, 14 x 153" (35.6 x 388.6 cm) overall
Collection of Audrey Strohl, courtesy Holly Solomon Gallery, New York, and Rosamund Felsen Gallery, Los Angeles

Joan Snyder

Untitled, 1980

God Bless the Child..., 1980
Mixed media on canvas, 72 x 120″
(182.9 x 304.8 cm)
Hamilton Gallery of Contemporary Art,
New York

Untitled, 1980
Mixed media on canvas, 60 x 120″
(152.4 x 304.8 cm)
Hamilton Gallery of Contemporary Art,
New York

Robert Snyder

Lines of Force, 1979

Lines of Force, 1979
Video, color, 12 minutes
Lent by the artist

Video Program III
Wednesday, February 4–Sunday,
April 12, daily at 1:15 and 5:15

Chick Strand

Still from *Loose Ends,* 1979

Loose Ends, 1979
Film, black and white, 25 minutes
Lent by the artist

Film Program VII
Friday, March 27–Sunday, April 12,
daily at 1:15; Tuesday, March 31, at 6:00

Wayne Thiebaud

Freeways, 1978–79

Freeways, 1978–79
Oil on canvas, 48 x 60″
(121.9 x 152.4 cm)
Private collection

San Francisco Freeways, 1980-81
Oil on canvas, 36 x 48″
(91.4 x 121.9 cm)
Lent by the artist, courtesy Allan Stone
Gallery, New York

Richard Thompson

That Awful Moment at the Rainbow's End Trailer Court (from "The Terrible Death Desert Storm"), 1980

Planet Family Portrait (from "The Death Desert Portrait Gallery"), 1980
Oil on canvas, 60 x 84″
(152.4 x 213.4 cm)
Monique Knowlton Gallery, New York

That Awful Moment at the Rainbow's End Trailer Court (from "The Terrible Death Desert Storm"), 1980
Oil on canvas, 60 x 96″
(152.4 x 243.8 cm)
Space, Los Angeles

Joan Thorne

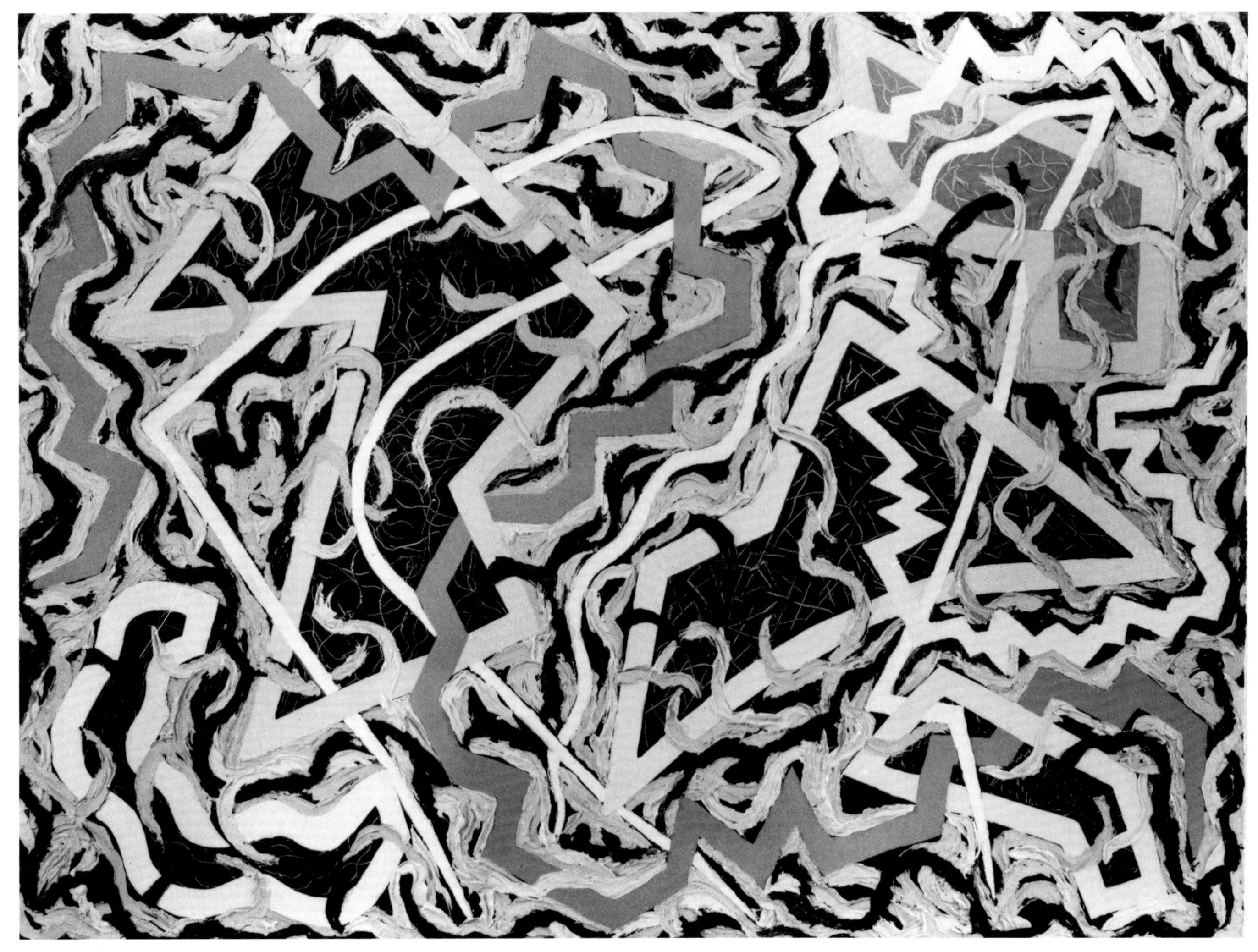

Avur, 1980

Avur, 1980
Oil on canvas, 75 x 103″
(190.5 x 261.6 cm)
Collection of Stefan Edlis

Mazu, 1980
Oil on canvas, 75 x 103″
(190.5 x 261.6 cm)
Collection of Mr. and
Mrs. David S. Solomon

Jack Tworkov

The Exes, 1980

The Ens, 1980
Oil on canvas, 57 x 84½″
(144.8 x 215 cm)
Lent by the artist, courtesy Nancy Hoffman Gallery, New York

The Exes, 1980
Oil on canvas, 57 x 84½″
(144.8 x 215 cm)
Lent by the artist, courtesy Nancy Hoffman Gallery, New York

William Viola

CHOTT el-DJERID (A Portrait in Light and Heat), 1979

CHOTT el-DJERID (A Portrait in Light and Heat), 1979
Video, color, 28 minutes
Electronic Arts Intermix, New York

Video Program I
Wednesday, February 4–Sunday, April 12, daily at 11:30 and 3:30

Russ Warren

Etla Noche, 1980

Etla Noche, 1980
Acrylic on canvas, 48 x 66″
(121.9 x 167.6 cm)
Lent by the artist

The Triumph of Death, 1980
Acrylic on canvas, 48 x 60″
(121.9 x 152.4 cm)
Lent by the artist

William Wegman

Polynesian (2), 1979

Polynesian (2), 1979
Color photograph, Polaroid, 24 x 20″
(61 x 50.8 cm)
Delahunty Gallery, Dallas

Ray Bat, 1980
Color photograph, Polaroid, 24 x 20″
(61 x 50.8 cm)
Private collection

Untitled, 1980
Color photograph, Polaroid, 24 x 20″
(61 x 50.8 cm)
Holly Solomon Gallery, New York

Robert Wilson

Act I set for *I Was Sitting On My Patio This Guy Appeared I Thought I Was Hallucinating*, Cherry Lane Theater, New York, 1977

Stage set from *I Was Sitting On My Patio This Guy Appeared I Thought I Was Hallucinating*, 1977–80
Props: *Light Table*, stainless steel, Plexiglas, electric light, 29 x 48½ x 15″ (73.7 x 123.2 x 38.1 cm); *Patio Sofa*, stainless steel, 32½ x 65½ x 18½ (82.6 x 166.4 x 47 cm); *Telephone Table*, stainless steel, 9 x 12½ x 12″ (22.9 x 31.8 x 30.5 cm); painted stage drop; fabric arches; flooring
Collection of Robert Wilson, Byrd Hoffman Foundation, New York

Robert Zakanitch

Hearts of Swan, 1980

Hearts of Swan, 1980
Acrylic on canvas, 88 x 192″
(223.5 x 487.8 cm)
Robert Miller Gallery, New York

Artists' Biographies

Vito Acconci

Born in the Bronx, New York, 1940
Studied at Holy Cross College, Worcester, Massachusetts (B.A., 1962); Writers Workshop, University of Iowa, Iowa City (M.F.A., 1964)
Lives in Brooklyn, New York

SELECTED INSTALLATIONS: John Gibson Gallery, New York, *Control Box,* 1971; Kassel, West Germany, Documenta 5, *Four support rooms for a performance,* 1972; Galleria Forma, Genoa, Italy, *Intermediaries,* 1973; Whitney Museum of American Art, New York, *Round-trip,* 1975; 37th Venice Biennale, *Venice Belongs to Us,* 1976; Whitney Museum of American Art, 1977 Biennial Exhibition, *Tonight We Escape from New York;* Museum of Contemporary Art, Chicago, "View of a Decade," *The Gangster Sister from Chicago,* 1977; Stedelijk Museum, Amsterdam, *Monument to the Dead Children,* 1978; Kunstverein Hamburg, West Germany, "The Artist: Hermit? Investigator? Social Worker?" *Let's Pretend That This is an Apparatus for a Political Kidnapping,* 1979; Galerie Sonnabend, Paris, *Exercise Machine for an Eternal Return,* 1980; Muhlenberg College Art Gallery, Allentown, Pennsylvania, *Instant House,* 1980.

Robert Adams

Born in Orange, New Jersey, 1937
Studied at the University of Redlands, Redlands, California (B.A., 1959); University of Southern California, Los Angeles (Ph.D., 1965)
Lives in Longmont, Colorado

SELECTED SOLO EXHIBITIONS: Colorado Springs Fine Arts Center, Colorado, 1971; Castelli Graphics, New York, 1976; Robert Self Gallery, London, 1978; The Denver Art Museum, 1978; The Museum of Modern Art, New York, 1979.

SELECTED GROUP EXHIBITIONS: The Museum of Modern Art, New York, "Photographs by Robert Adams and Emmet Gowin," 1971; The Metropolitan Museum of Art, New York, "Landscape/Cityscape," 1973; The Baltimore Museum of Art, "14 American Photographers," 1975 (traveled nationally); The Museum of Fine Arts, Houston, "Contemporary American Photographic Works," 1977 (traveled nationally); The Museum of Modern Art, New York, "Mirrors and Windows: American Photography Since 1960," 1978 (traveled nationally); Corcoran Gallery of Art, Washington, D.C., "American Images," 1979 (traveled nationally).

Gregory Amenoff

Born in St. Charles, Illinois, 1948
Studied at Beloit College, Beloit, Wisconsin (B.A., 1970)
Lives in New York

SELECTED SOLO EXHIBITIONS: Brockton Art Center, Fuller Memorial, Brockton, Massachusetts, 1972; Hayden Gallery, Massachusetts Institute of Technology, Cambridge, 1976; Nielsen Gallery, Boston, 1977, 1978, 1980.

SELECTED GROUP EXHIBITIONS: City Hall, Boston, "Boston Visual Artists Union First Annual City Hall Exhibition," 1971; Boston Visual Artists Union, "Affinities," 1974; Institute of Contemporary Art, Boston, "Painted in Boston," 1975; Brockton Art Center, Fuller Memorial, Brockton, Massachusetts, "Painting Invitational," 1975; "13 Boston Artists," 1975 (organized by the United States Information Agency, Washington, D.C.; traveled internationally); Institute of Contemporary Art, Boston, "Boston 200 Bicentennial Exhibition," 1976; Brockton Art Center, Fuller Memorial, "Art Treasures of New England," 1977; Institute of Contemporary Art of The University of Pennsylvania, Philadelphia, "Eight Abstract Painters," 1978; Rose Art Museum, Brandeis University, Waltham, Massachusetts, "Art of the State," 1979; Brockton Art Center, Fuller Memorial, "Aspects of the '70s: Painterly Abstraction," 1980; Neuberger Museum, State University of New York, College at Purchase, "Seven Artists," 1980.

William Anastasi

Born in Philadelphia, 1933
Studied at Temple University, Philadelphia (1952–53); University of Pennsylvania, Philadelphia (1954–61)
Lives in New York

SELECTED SOLO EXHIBITIONS: Dwan Gallery, New York, 1965, 1967, 1970; The Hudson River Museum, Yonkers, New York, 1979; Kunstmuseum Düsseldorf, West Germany, 1979.

SELECTED GROUP EXHIBITIONS: Dwan Gallery, New York, "Language I," 1966; Musée d'Art Moderne de la Ville de Paris, "Artistes et Découvreurs de Notre Temps," 1970; Musée Cantonal des Beaux-Arts, Lausanne, Switzerland, "3e Salon International des Galeries Pilotes," 1970; Whitney Museum of American Art, New York, New American Filmmakers Series, "Re-Visions: Projects and Proposals in Film and Video," 1979; Akademie der Künste, West Berlin, "Für Augen und Ohren," 1980; Musée d'Art Moderne de la Ville de Paris, "Écouter par les Yeux," 1980.

Kenneth Anger

Born in 1930
Lives in New York

SELECTED SOLO EXHIBITIONS: Whitney Museum of American Art, New York, New American Filmmakers Series, 1975; Collective for Living Cinema, New York, 1979; Image, Atlanta, 1979; Laguna Gloria Art Museum, Austin, Texas, 1979.

Siah Armajani

Born in Teheran, Iran, 1939
Studied at Macalester College, St. Paul, Minnesota (B.A., 1963)
Lives in Minneapolis

SELECTED SOLO EXHIBITIONS: The Clocktower, Institute for Art and Urban Resources, New York, 1974; Philadelphia College of Art, 1978; Max Protetch Gallery, New York, 1978; Ohio State University, Columbus, 1979; Contemporary Arts Center, Cincinnati, 1980; Joslyn Art Museum, Omaha, Nebraska, 1980.

SELECTED GROUP EXHIBITIONS: Museum of Contemporary Art, Chicago, "Art by Telephone," 1969; The Museum of Modern Art, New York, "Information," 1970; Walker Art Center, Minneapolis, "Works for New Spaces," 1971; Kassel, West Germany, Documenta 5, 1972; Carpenter Center for the Visual Arts, Harvard University, Cambridge, Massachusetts, "Virtual Reality," 1976; Walker Art Center, "Scale and Environment: 10 Sculptors," 1977; The Solomon R. Guggenheim Museum, New York, "Young American Artists," 1978; Whitney Museum of American Art, Downtown Branch, New York, "Architectural Analogues," 1978; Wave Hill, Bronx, New York, "Wave Hill: The Artist's View," 1979; 39th Venice Biennale, 1980; Los Angeles Institute of Contemporary Art, "Architectural Sculpture," 1980; Institute of Contemporary Art of The University of Pennsylvania, Philadelphia, "Drawings: The Pluralist Decade," 1980; XIII Winter Olympic Games, Lake Placid, New York, "Environmental Art," 1980.

Charles Arnoldi

Born in Dayton, Ohio, 1946
Studied at Chouinard Art Institute, Los Angeles (1968)
Lives in Venice, California

SELECTED SOLO EXHIBITIONS: Riko Mizuno Gallery, Los Angeles, 1971; Texas Gallery, Houston, 1972; Nicholas Wilder Gallery, Los Angeles, 1974; Robert Elkon Gallery, New York, 1975; Nicholas Wilder Gallery, 1975; Seattle Art Museum, 1976; Nicholas Wilder Gallery, 1977; Texas Gallery, 1977; Robert Elkon Gallery, 1978; Nicholas Wilder Gallery, 1978; Texas Gallery, 1979; Nicholas Wilder Gallery, 1979; Dobrick Gallery, Chicago, 1979; Robert Elkon Gallery, 1979; James Corcoran Gallery, Los Angeles, 1979.

SELECTED GROUP EXHIBITIONS: Museum of Contemporary Art, Chicago, "Permutations: Light and Color," 1969; Kassel, West Germany, Documenta 5, 1972;

San Francisco Museum of Modern Art, "Painting and Sculpture in California: The Modern Era," 1976 (traveled nationally).

Alice Aycock

Born in Harrisburg, Pennsylvania, 1946
Studied at Douglass College, Rutgers University, New Brunswick, New Jersey (B.A., 1968); Hunter College, New York (M.A., 1971)
Lives in New York

SELECTED SOLO EXHIBITIONS: Nova Scotia College of Art and Design, Halifax, 1972; 112 Green Street Gallery, New York, 1974; Artpark, Lewiston, New York, 1977; The Museum of Modern Art, New York, 1977; John Weber Gallery, New York, 1978; Cranbrook Academy of Art/Museum, Bloomfield Hills, Michigan, 1978; Contemporary Arts Center, Cincinnati, 1979; P.S. 1, Institute for Art and Urban Resources, Long Island City, New York, 1980; Fort Worth Art Museum, 1980.

SELECTED GROUP EXHIBITIONS: Kassel, West Germany, Documenta 6, 1977; John Weber Gallery, New York, "Drawings for Outdoor Sculpture, 1946–77," 1977; Stedelijk Museum, Amsterdam, "Made by Sculptors," 1978; 38th Venice Biennale, 1978; Whitney Museum of American Art, New York, 1979 Biennial Exhibition; Battery Park City Landfill, New York, "Art On the Beach," 1980; 39th Venice Biennale, 1980.

William Bailey

Born in Council Bluffs, Iowa, 1930
Studied at the School of Fine Arts, University of Kansas, Lawrence (1948–51); School of Art and Architecture, Yale University, New Haven, Connecticut (B.F.A., 1955; M.F.A., 1957)
Lives in New Haven, Connecticut

SELECTED SOLO EXHIBITIONS: Robert Hull Fleming Museum, University of Vermont, Burlington, 1956; Kanegis Gallery, Boston, 1957, 1958, 1961; Indiana University Art Museum, Bloomington, 1963; Kansas City Art Institute, Kansas City, Missouri, 1967; Robert Schoelkopf Gallery, New York, 1968, 1971; Galleria dei Lanzi, Milan, 1973; Galleria Il Fante di Spade, Rome, 1973; Robert Schoelkopf Gallery, 1974; Galerie Claude Bernard, Paris, 1978; Robert Schoelkopf Gallery, 1979; Il Gabbiano Galleria, Rome, 1980.

SELECTED GROUP EXHIBITIONS: Institute of Contemporary Art, Boston, "Selection 1957," 1957; Contemporary Arts Museum, Houston, "Image and Idea," 1960; Vassar College Art Gallery, Poughkeepsie, New York, "Realism Now," 1968; Whitney Museum of American Art, New York, "22 Realists," 1970 (traveled nationally); Yale University Art Gallery, New Haven, Connecticut, "Seven Realists," 1973; Montgomery Museum of Fine Arts, Montgomery, Alabama, "American Painting of the 60s and 70s: The Real, The Ideal, The Fantastic," 1979 (traveled nationally); Whitney Museum of American Art, "The Figurative Tradition and the Whitney Museum of American Art," 1980.

Jennifer Bartlett

Born in Long Beach, California, 1941
Studied at Mills College, Oakland, California (B.A., 1963); School of Art and Architecture, Yale University, New Haven, Connecticut (B.F.A., 1964; M.F.A., 1965)
Lives in New York

SELECTED SOLO EXHIBITIONS: Mills College, Oakland, California, 1963; 119 Spring Street Gallery, New York, 1970; Reese Palley Gallery, New York, 1972; Paula Cooper Gallery, New York, 1974, 1976; Contemporary Arts Center, Cincinnati, 1976; Wadsworth Atheneum, Hartford, Connecticut, 1977; Art Gallery, University of California, Irvine, 1978; Hansen Fuller Gallery, San Francisco, 1978; Margo Leavin Gallery, Los Angeles, 1979; The Clocktower, Institute for Art and Urban Resources, New York, 1979; Galerie Mukai, Tokyo, 1980; Akron Art Institute, Akron, Ohio, 1980.

Bartlett *(cont.)*

SELECTED GROUP EXHIBITIONS: The Museum of Modern Art, New York, "Seven Walls," 1971; Whitney Museum of American Art, New York, "Annual Exhibition: Contemporary American Painting," 1972; Whitney Museum of American Art, "Contemporary American Drawings," 1973; Corcoran Gallery of Art, Washington, D.C., 37th Corcoran Biennial, 1975; 9e Biennale de Paris, 1975; Aarhus Kunstmuseum, Aarhus, Denmark, "The Liberation: Fourteen American Artists," 1976 (traveled internationally); Akademie der Künste, West Berlin, "Soho," 1976; Whitney Museum of American Art, 1977 Biennial Exhibition; Kassel, West Germany, Documenta 6, 1977; New York State Museum, Albany, "New York: The State of Art," 1977; Whitney Museum of American Art, "New Image Painting," 1978; Whitney Museum of American Art, 1979 Biennial Exhibition; 39th Venice Biennale, 1980.

Lynda Benglis

Born in Lake Charles, Louisiana, 1941
Studied at Newcomb College, New Orleans (B.F.A., 1964)
Lives in New York

SELECTED SOLO EXHIBITIONS: Paula Cooper Gallery, New York, 1970, 1971; Hayden Gallery, Massachusetts Institute of Technology, Cambridge, 1971; Hansen Fuller Gallery, San Francisco, 1972, 1973; The Clocktower, Institute for Art and Urban Resources, New York, 1973; Paula Cooper Gallery, 1974, 1975; The Kitchen Center for Video, Music and Dance, New York, 1975; Paula Cooper Gallery, 1976; Margo Leavin Gallery, Los Angeles, 1977; Paula Cooper Gallery, 1978; Texas Gallery, Houston, 1979, 1980; Paula Cooper Gallery, 1980.

SELECTED GROUP EXHIBITIONS: Finch College Museum, New York, "Art and Process IV," 1969; Walker Art Center, Minneapolis, "Works For New Spaces," 1971; Whitney Museum of American Art, New York, 1973 Biennial Exhibition; The Baltimore Museum of Art, "Fourteen Artists," 1975; New Orleans Museum of Art, "Five from Louisiana," 1977; Stedelijk Museum, Amsterdam, "Made by Sculptors," 1978; The Museum of Modern Art, New York, "Contemporary Sculpture: Selections from the Collection of The Museum of Modern Art," 1979; Whitney Museum of American Art, Downtown Branch, "Painting in Relief," 1980; San Diego Museum of Art, "Sculpture in California, 1975–80," 1980; Museum of Contemporary Art, Chicago, "3 Dimensional Painting," 1980; 39th Venice Biennale, 1980; Institute of Contemporary Art of The University of Pennsylvania, Philadelphia, "Drawings: The Pluralist Decade," 1980.

James Benning

Born in Milwaukee, Wisconsin, 1942
Studied at the University of Wisconsin, Milwaukee (M.S., 1970); University of Wisconsin, Madison (M.F.A., 1975)
Lives in New York

SELECTED SOLO EXHIBITIONS: Film Forum, New York, 1973; Museum of Contemporary Art, Chicago, 1975; The Museum of Modern Art, New York, 1976; Walker Art Center, Minneapolis, 1977; The Art Institute of Chicago Film Center, 1977; Pacific Film Archive, University Art Museum, Berkeley, California, 1977; San Francisco Museum of Modern Art, 1977; Collective for Living Cinema, New York, 1977; Boston Film/Video Foundation, 1978; Albright-Knox Art Gallery, Buffalo, New York, 1978; Whitney Museum of American Art, New York, New American Filmmakers Series, 1978, 1979; Institute of Contemporary Art, Boston, 1980; The Museum of Modern Art, New York, 1980.

SELECTED GROUP EXHIBITIONS: Cannes International Film Festival, 1974; The Museum of Modern Art, New York, "New Directors/New Films," 1975, 1977; Edinburgh International Film Festival, 1977; Ann Arbor Film Festival, University of Michigan, 1977; Edinburgh International Film Festival, 1978; Walker Art Center, Minneapolis, "Eight Artists—The Elusive Image," 1979; Whitney Museum of American Art, New York, 1979 Biennial Exhibition; Edinburgh International Film Festival, 1980.

Jonathan Borofsky

Born in Boston, 1942
Studied at Carnegie-Mellon University, Pittsburgh (B.F.A., 1964); Fontainebleau School of Fine Arts, Palais de Fontainebleau, France (1964); School of Art and Architecture, Yale University, New Haven, Connecticut (M.F.A., 1966)
Lives in Venice, California

SELECTED SOLO EXHIBITIONS: Paula Cooper Gallery, New York, 1975; Wadsworth Atheneum, Hartford, Connecticut, 1976; Paula Cooper Gallery, 1976; Art Gallery, University of California, Irvine, 1977; Protetch-McIntosh Gallery, Washington, D.C., 1978; University Art Museum, University of California, Berkeley, 1978; The Museum of Modern Art, New York, 1978; Paula Cooper Gallery, 1979; Halle für Internationale Neue Kunst, Zurich, 1979; Portland Center for the Visual Arts, Portland, Oregon, 1979; Paula Cooper Gallery, 1980.

SELECTED GROUP EXHIBITIONS: Whitney Museum of American Art, New York, Downtown Branch, "Autogeography," 1975; Fine Arts Building, New York, "Style and Process," 1976; 37th Venice Biennale, 1976; New York State Museum, Albany, "New York: The State of Art," 1977; Protetch-McIntosh Gallery, Washington, D.C., "Minimal Image," 1978; Whitney Museum of American Art, 1979 Biennial Exhibition; Renaissance Society at the University of Chicago, "Visionary Images," 1979; Neuberger Museum, State University of New York, College at Purchase, "Ten Artists/Artists Space," 1979; 39th Venice Biennale, 1980.

Stan Brakhage

Born in Kansas City, Missouri, 1933
Studied at Dartmouth College, Hanover, New Hampshire (1950–51); Institute of Fine Arts, San Francisco (1952)
Lives in Rollinsville, Colorado

SELECTED SOLO EXHIBITIONS: The Museum of Modern Art, New York, 1971; Anthology Film Archives, New York, 1974, 1975; Whitney Museum of American Art, New York, New American Filmmakers Series, 1975, 1977; The Museum of Modern Art, New York, 1977; Anthology Film Archives, 1977; Collective for Living Cinema, New York, 1977, 1979, 1980; Whitney Museum of American Art, New American Filmmakers Series, 1980.

SELECTED GROUP EXHIBITIONS: The Museum of Modern Art, New York, "American Independent Cinema: Recent Acquisitions," 1979; Collective for Living Cinema, New York, "New and Recent Films," 1979; Whitney Museum of American Art, New York, 1979 Biennial Exhibition.

Robert Breer

Born in Detroit, 1926
Studied at Stanford University, Stanford, California (B.A., 1949)
Lives in South Nyack, New York

SELECTED SOLO EXHIBITIONS: Palais des Beaux-Arts, Brussels, 1956; Charles Cinema, New York, 1961; Bleecker Street Cinema, New York, 1962; Dwan Gallery, Los Angeles, 1963; Galeria Bonino, New York, 1965, 1966; Museum of Contemporary Art, Chicago, 1969; The Museum of Modern Art, New York, 1970; Millennium Film Workshop, New York, 1972; Michael Berger Gallery, Pittsburgh, 1974; The Museum of Modern Art, New York, 1975; Film Forum, New York, 1975; Whitney Museum of American Art, New York, New American Filmmakers Series, 1975, 1977, 1980.

SELECTED GROUP EXHIBITIONS: Stedelijk Museum, Amsterdam, "International Exhibition of Art in Motion," 1961; Gallery of Modern Art, New York, "The Contemporary Avant-Garde," 1964; The National Museum of Modern Art, Tokyo, "The American Experimental Film," 1967; Whitney Museum of American Art, New York, New American Filmmakers Series, "Twelve Short Trips," 1971, "An Animation Festival," 1972; Yale University, New Haven, Connecticut, "Options and Alternatives," 1973; Montreux, Switzerland, "New Forms in Film," 1974; Whitney Museum of American Art, "Color Abstraction: Film," 1978; Whitney Museum of American Art, 1979 Biennial Exhibition.

Michael Brewster

Born in Eugene, Oregon, 1946
Studied at Pomona College, Claremont, California (B.A., 1968); Claremont Graduate School, Pomona (M.F.A., 1970)
Lives in Venice, California

SELECTED INSTALLATIONS: Mojave Desert, California, *Configuration 006*, 1969; Montgomery Gallery, Pomona College, Claremont, California, *Configuration 010*, 1970; F Space, Santa Ana, California, *Number 013*, 1971; University of Victoria, Victoria, British Columbia, *The Field Contained by Room 094*, 1976; Artists Space, New York, *An Acoustic Sculpture and a Clicker Drawing*, 1977; La Jolla Museum of Contemporary Art, La Jolla, California, *Synchromesh*, 1978; Cirrus Gallery, Los Angeles, *Surrounded: Sharp Points Ringing*, 1979.

SELECTED GROUP EXHIBITIONS: Newport Harbor Art Museum, Newport Beach, California, "Sounds Show," 1976; Fort Worth Art Museum, "Los Angeles in the Seventies," 1977 (traveled nationally); Los Angeles Institute of Contemporary Art, "Sound," 1979; P.S. 1, Institute for Art and Urban Resources, Long Island City, New York, "Sound at P.S. 1," 1979.

Barbara Buckner

Born in Chicago, 1950
Studied at Boston College (1968–70); New York University, Institute of Film and Television (B.F.A., 1972)
Lives in New York

SELECTED SOLO EXHIBITIONS: The Kitchen Center for Video, Music and Dance, New York, 1973, 1974; Anthology Film Archives, New York, 1975, 1976, 1977; Collective for Living Cinema, New York, 1977; The Museum of Modern Art, New York, 1977; Experimental Television Center, Binghamton, New York, 1978; Media Study, Buffalo, New York, 1978; Holly Solomon Gallery, New York, 1979; Boston Film/Video Foundation, 1979; The Art Institute of Chicago, 1980; Ithaca Video Projects, New York, 1980; Visual Studies Workshop, Rochester, New York, 1980; Media Study, 1980; Whitney Museum of American Art, New York, New American Filmmakers Series, 1980.

SELECTED GROUP EXHIBITIONS: Yale Film Festival, New York, 1972; Whitney Museum of American Art, New York, New American Filmmakers Series, "Far Out," 1972; 10th Annual Avant-Garde Festival, New York, 1973; Video Expovision, Woodstock, New York, 1975, 1976; Williams College Museum of Art, Williamstown, Massachusetts, "Open Stacks," 1977; Everson Museum of Art, Syracuse, New York, "Revue," 1979; Whitney Museum of American Art, 1979 Biennial Exhibition; The Kitchen Center for Video, Music and Dance, New York, "Image Processed Tapes," 1979, 1980; American Center, Paris, "Video from the Program of The Museum of Modern Art," 1980.

Scott Burton

Born in Greensboro, Alabama, 1939
Studied at Columbia University, New York (B.A., 1962); New York University (M.A., 1963)
Lives in New York

SELECTED SOLO EXHIBITIONS: Artists Space, New York, 1975; Droll/Kolbert Gallery, New York, 1977; Brooks Jackson Iolas Gallery, New York, 1978; Protetch-McIntosh Gallery, Washington, D.C., 1979; Daniel Weinberg Gallery, San Francisco, 1980.

SELECTED GROUP EXHIBITIONS: Allen Memorial Art Museum, Oberlin, Ohio, "Festival of Contemporary Arts," 1973; Whitney Museum of American Art, New York, 1975 Biennial Exhibition; Institute of Contemporary Art of The University of Pennsylvania, Philadelphia, "Improbable Furniture," 1977 (traveled nationally); The Solomon R. Guggenheim Museum, New York, "Young American Artists," 1978; Neuberger Museum, State University of New York, College at Purchase, "Ten Artists/Artists Space," 1979; The Detroit Institute of Arts, "Image and Object in Contemporary Sculpture," 1979; Art Gallery, Otis Art Institute, Los Angeles, "Furnishings by Artists," 1980.

SELECTED PERFORMANCES: Wadsworth Atheneum, Hartford, Connecticut, "Four Theater Pieces," 1970; Whitney Museum of American Art, New York, "Group Behavior Tableaux," 1972; Artists Space, New York, "Persona," 1974; The Solomon R. Guggenheim Museum, New York, "Pair Behavior Tableaux," 1976; Kassel, West Germany, Documenta 6, 1977; University Art Museum, University of California, Berkeley, "Individual Behavior Tableaux," 1980.

Harry Callahan

Born in Detroit, 1912
Studied at Michigan State University, East Lansing (1936–38)
Lives in Providence, Rhode Island

SELECTED SOLO EXHIBITIONS: 750 Studio Gallery, Chicago, 1946; The Art Institute of Chicago, 1951; Kansas City Art Institute, Missouri, 1956; International Museum of Photography at George Eastman House, Rochester, New York, 1958; The Museum of Modern Art, New York, 1968 (traveled nationally); Witkin Gallery, New York, 1970; The Museum of Modern Art, New York, 1976; Galerie Zabriskie, Paris, 1977; Light Gallery, New York, 1980.

SELECTED GROUP EXHIBITIONS: The Museum of Modern Art, New York, "In and Out of Focus," 1948; The Museum of Modern Art, New York, "50 Photographs by 50 Photographers," 1948; Los Angeles County Museum of Art, "Photography at Mid-Century," 1950; The Museum of Modern Art, New York, "The Family of Man," 1955 (traveled internationally); 28th Venice Biennale, 1956; 38th Venice Biennale, 1978; Corcoran Gallery of Art, Washington, D.C., "American Images," 1979 (traveled nationally).

Jo Ann Callis

Born in Cincinnati, 1940
Studied at the University of California, Los Angeles (B.A., 1974; M.F.A., 1977)
Lives in Culver City, California

SELECTED SOLO EXHIBITIONS: Grandview Gallery, Woman's Building, Los Angeles, 1974; Tyler School of Art, Temple University, Philadelphia, 1975; Orange Coast College, Costa Mesa, California, 1975, 1978; Gallery of Fine Photography, New Orleans, 1978; Image Gallery, Aarhus, Denmark, 1980; G. Ray Hawkins Gallery, Los Angeles, 1980.

SELECTED GROUP EXHIBITIONS: Mills House, Garden Grove, California, "Eight Los Angeles Photographers," 1975; Friends of Photography, Carmel, California, "Emerging Los Angeles Photographers," 1976; Tasmania, Australia, "International Invitational Australian Arts Festival," 1977; The Art Galleries, California State University, Long Beach, "The Photograph as Artifice," 1978; G. Ray Hawkins Gallery, Los Angeles, "Interrogations into Color," 1978; University Art Museum, University of California, Berkeley, "Color Transformations," 1979; University of Hawaii, Honolulu, "Spectrum—New Directions in Color Photography," 1979 (traveled nationally); Fogg Art Museum, Harvard University, Cambridge, Massachusetts, "Contemporary Photographs," 1980.

Louisa Chase

Born in Panama City, Panama, 1951
Studied at Yale University Summer School of Music and Art, Norfolk, Connecticut (1971); Syracuse University, Syracuse, New York (B.F.A., 1973); School of Art and Architecture, Yale University, New Haven, Connecticut (M.F.A., 1975)
Lives in New York

SELECTED SOLO EXHIBITIONS: Artists Space, New York, 1975; Edward Thorp Gallery, New York, 1977; Woods Gerry Gallery, Rhode Island School of Design, Providence, 1977; Swarthmore Art Gallery, Swarthmore, Pennsylvania, 1978; Edward Thorp Gallery, 1978.

SELECTED GROUP EXHIBITIONS: Webb and Parsons Gallery, Bedford, New York, 1974; Edward Thorp Gallery, New York, 1976; Museum of Art, Rhode Island School of Design, Providence, "Rhode Island School of Design Faculty Exhibition,"

Chase *(cont.)*

1977; Grey Art Gallery, New York University, "Painting of the Eighties," 1979; Max Protetch Gallery, New York, "Re:Figuration," 1979; The New Museum, New York, "New Work/New York," 1979.

Christo

Born in Gabrovo, Bulgaria, 1935
Studied at Fine Arts Academy, Sofia, Bulgaria (1952–56); Burian Theater, Prague (1956); Vienna Fine Arts Academy (1957)
Lives in New York

Selected Solo Exhibitions and Installations: Galerie Haro Lauhus, Cologne, West Germany, 1961; Galerie Schmela, Düsseldorf, West Germany, 1963; Leo Castelli Gallery, New York, 1966; Walker Art Center, Minneapolis, 1966; Institute of Contemporary Art of The University of Pennsylvania, Philadelphia, 1968; Museum of Contemporary Art, Chicago, 1969; Kaiser Wilhelm Museum, Krefeld, West Germany, 1970; Rifle, Colorado, *Valley Curtain*, 1970 (site installation); The Museum of Fine Arts, Houston, 1971; Grand Hogback, Rifle, Colorado, *Valley Curtain, Grand Hogback, Rifle, Colorado*, 1971 (site installation); Stedelijk Museum, Amsterdam, 1973; Marin County, California, *Running Fence*, 1973 (site installation); Louisiana Museum, Humlebaek, Denmark, 1974; Museum Boymans van Beuningen, Rotterdam, 1977; William Rockhill Nelson Gallery and Atkins Museum of Fine Arts, Kansas City, Missouri, 1978; Corcoran Gallery of Art, Washington, D.C., 1979; Newport Harbor Art Museum, Newport Beach, California, 1980.

Larry Clark

Born in Tulsa, Oklahoma, 1943
Studied at Layton School of Art, Milwaukee, Wisconsin (1961–62)
Lives in New York

Selected Solo Exhibitions: San Francisco Art Institute, 1971: University of North Dakota, Grand Forks, 1972; Kirkland College, Clinton, New York, 1973; State University of New York, Buffalo, 1973; Oakton College, California, 1973; International Museum of Photography at George Eastman House, Rochester, New York, 1975 (traveled internationally); New School of Photography, New York, 1976; Robert Freidus Gallery, New York, 1979; Photographers' Gallery and Workshop, South Yarra, Australia, 1979; James Madison University, Harrisonburg, Virginia, 1980; Glyth Gallery, Amherst, Massachusetts, 1980; Robert Freidus Gallery, 1980.

Selected Group Exhibitions: Corcoran Gallery of Art, Washington, D.C., "The Collection of Sam Wagstaff," 1978 (traveled nationally); De Cordova and Dana Museum and Park, Lincoln, Massachusetts, "Photography: Recent Directions," 1980.

Robert Cumming

Born in Worcester, Massachusetts, 1943
Studied at the Massachusetts College of Art, Boston (B.F.A., 1965); University of Illinois, Champaign-Urbana (M.F.A., 1967)
Lives in West Suffield, Connecticut

Selected Solo Exhibitions: Phoenix College, Phoenix, Arizona, 1973; Los Angeles Institute of Contemporary Art, 1976; Friends of Photography, Carmel, California, 1979; Institute of Modern Art, Brisbane, Australia, 1979 (traveled); Rhode Island School of Design, Providence, 1980.

Selected Group Exhibitions: The Art Institute of Chicago, "Chicago and Vicinity," 1969; Museum of Contemporary Art, Chicago, "Art by Telephone," 1969; The Detroit Institute of Arts, "Other Ideas," 1969; Whitney Museum of American Art, New York, 1977 Biennial Exhibition; The Museum of Modern Art, New York, "Mirrors and Windows: American Photography Since 1960," 1978.

Peter D'Agostino

Born in New York, 1945
Studied at The Art Students League of New York (1963–64); Academy of Fine

Arts, Naples (1965–66); School of Visual Arts, New York (B.F.A., 1968); San Francisco State University (M.A., 1975)
Lives in New York

SELECTED SOLO EXHIBITIONS: 80 Langton Street, San Francisco, 1975; San Francisco Museum of Modern Art, 1977; Artists Space, New York, 1978; Ohio State University, Columbus, 1978; Contemporary Arts Center, Cincinnati, 1979; Washington Project for the Arts, Washington, D.C., 1979; Long Beach Museum of Art, California, 1979; The Museum of Modern Art, New York, 1979; Los Angeles Institute of Contemporary Art, 1980.

SELECTED GROUP EXHIBITIONS: Aarhus Kunstmuseum, Aarhus, Denmark, "Video International," 1976; Museum of Modern Art, Bologna, Italy, "Week of International Performance," 1977; San Francisco Museum of Modern Art, "Space/Time/Sound—1970's: A Decade in the Bay Area," 1979; Athens Video Festival, Athens, Ohio, 1979; Everson Museum of Art, Syracuse, New York, and The Kitchen Center for Video, Music and Dance, New York, "Ithaca Video Festival," 1979; College of Architecture, Barcelona, "Video: Time and Space," 1980; San Francisco Video Festival, "Video 80," 1980.

Willem de Kooning

Born in Rotterdam, 1904
Studied at the Academie voor Beeldende Kunsten en Technische Wetenschappen, Rotterdam (1916–25); Académie Royale des Beaux-Arts, Brussels (1924); Van Schelling Design School, Antwerp (1924)
Lives in The Springs, Long Island, New York

SELECTED SOLO EXHIBITIONS: Egan Gallery, New York, 1948, 1951; Sidney Janis Gallery, New York, 1953; Allan Stone Gallery, New York, 1964; Smith College Museum of Art, Northampton, Massachusetts, 1965 (traveled nationally); The Museum of Modern Art, New York, organizer, 1969 (traveled internationally); Sidney Janis Gallery, 1972; Walker Art Center, Minneapolis, 1974 (traveled nationally); Xavier Fourcade, Inc., New York, 1976; The Arts Council of Great Britain, London, organizer, 1977 (traveled internationally); The Solomon R. Guggenheim Museum, New York, 1978; Xavier Fourcade, Inc., 1979; Museum of Art, Carnegie Institute, Pittsburgh, 1979.

SELECTED GROUP EXHIBITIONS: McMillen Gallery, New York, 1942; Whitney Museum of American Art, New York, "Annual Exhibition of Contemporary American Sculpture, Watercolors and Drawings," 1948; Kootz Gallery, New York, "The Introspectives," 1949; Whitney Museum of American Art, "Annual Exhibition of Contemporary American Watercolors and Drawings," 1950; The Art Institute of Chicago, "60th Annual American Exhibition," 1951; 27th Venice Biennale, 1954; Whitney Museum of American Art, "The New Decade," 1955; Brussels World's Fair, "International Exhibition of Modern Art," 1958; Whitney Museum of American Art, "Annual Exhibition: Contemporary American Painting," 1963; Los Angeles County Museum of Art, "New York School: The First Generation. Paintings of the 1940's and 1950's," 1965; Whitney Museum of American Art, "Annual Exhibition: Contemporary American Painting," 1965, 1967; The Metropolitan Museum of Art, New York, "New York Painting and Sculpture: 1940–1970," 1969; Whitney Museum of American Art, "Annual Exhibition: Contemporary American Painting," 1972; The Art Institute of Chicago, "Seventy-second American Exhibition," 1976.

Richard Diebenkorn

Born in Portland, Oregon, 1922
Studied at Stanford University, Palo Alto, California (1940–43); University of California, Berkeley (1943–44); California School of Fine Arts, San Francisco (1946); Stanford University (B.A., 1949); University of New Mexico, Albuquerque (M.A., 1952)
Lives in Santa Monica, California

SELECTED SOLO EXHIBITIONS: California Palace of the Legion of Honor, San Francisco, 1948; Poindexter Gallery, New York, 1956, 1958; Pasadena Art Museum, California, 1960; The Phillips Collection, Washington, D.C., 1961; Gallery of

Diebenkorn *(cont.)*

Modern Art, Washington, D.C., 1964; Los Angeles County Museum of Art, 1969; Marlborough Gallery, New York, 1971; San Francisco Museum of Art, 1972; Albright-Knox Art Gallery, Buffalo, New York, 1976 (traveled nationally); M. Knoedler and Company, New York, 1977, 1979, 1980.

SELECTED GROUP EXHIBITIONS: The Solomon R. Guggenheim Museum, New York "Younger American Painters," 1954; Whitney Museum of American Art, New York, "Annual Exhibition: Contemporary American Painting," 1955; III Bienal International de São Paulo, Brazil, 1955; The Oakland Museum, California, "Contemporary Bay Area Figurative Painting," 1957 (traveled nationally); The Museum of Modern Art, New York, "New Images of Man," 1959; Whitney Museum of American Art, "Fifty California Artists," 1962 (traveled nationally); Tate Gallery, London, "Painting and Sculpture of a Decade," 1964; 34th Venice Biennale, 1968; The Arts Council of Great Britain-Hayward Gallery, London, "11 Los Angeles Artists," 1971; Albright-Knox Art Gallery, Buffalo, New York, "Heritage and Horizon: American Painting 1776–1976," 1976 (traveled nationally); 38th Venice Biennale, 1978; Albright-Knox Art Gallery, "American Paintings of the 1970s," 1978 (traveled nationally).

John Divola

Born in Santa Monica, California, 1949
Studied at California State University, Northridge (B.A., 1971); University of California, Los Angeles (M.A., 1973; M.F.A., 1974)
Lives in Venice, California

SELECTED SOLO EXHIBITIONS: Center for Creative Photography, University of Arizona, Tucson, 1976; Camera Work Gallery, Cincinnati, 1977; Image Gallery, Aarhus, Denmark, 1978; Los Angeles Institute of Contemporary Art, 1978.

SELECTED GROUP EXHIBITIONS: San Francisco Museum of Art, "24 from L.A.," 1973; Jack Glenn Gallery, Newport Beach, California, "Photography II," 1975; Light Gallery, New York, "Summer Light," 1975; Visual Studies Workshop, Rochester, New York, "Linda Connor, John Divola, Eric Renner," 1975; Arts Center, San Francisco, "West Coast Conceptual Photographers," 1976; The Art Galleries, California State University, Long Beach, "Beyond the Artist's Hand: Explorations of Change," 1976; Los Angeles Institute of Contemporary Art, "Exposing: Photographic Definitions," 1976; Friends of Photography, Carmel, California, "Emerging Los Angeles Photographers," 1977 (traveled nationally); The Museum of Modern Art, New York, "Mirrors and Windows: American Photography Since 1960," 1978; The Museum of Fine Arts, Houston, "Contemporary American Photographic Works," 1978; Visual Studies Workshop, Rochester, "John Divola, James Henkel, Burt Parker, John Pfahl," 1978 (traveled nationally).

Rackstraw Downes

Born in Pembury, Kent, England, 1939
Studied at Cambridge University, Cambridge, England (B.A., 1961); Yale University, New Haven, Connecticut (M.F.A., 1964); University of Pennsylvania, Philadelphia (1964–65)
Lives in New York

SELECTED SOLO EXHIBITIONS: Swarthmore College, Swarthmore, Pennsylvania, 1969; Kornblee Gallery, New York, 1972, 1974, 1975, 1978; Swain School of Design, New Bedford, Massachusetts, 1978; Tatistcheff and Company, New York, 1980; Kornblee Gallery, 1980.

SELECTED GROUP EXHIBITIONS: The Art Institute of Chicago, "Painterly Realism," 1972; Squibb Gallery, Princeton, New Jersey, "New Images in American Figurative Painting," 1975; Wave Hill, Bronx, New York, "The Landscape: Different Points of View," 1978; Brainerd Art Gallery, State University of New York, College at Potsdam, "Landscape/Cityscape," 1978; Lehigh University, Bethlehem, Pennsylvania, "Revival of Realism," 1979; Thorpe Intermedia Gallery, Sparkhill, New York, "New York Realists, 1980," 1980; Hartford Art School of the University of Hartford, West Hartford, Connecticut, "The Figurative Image," 1980.

Benni Efrat

Born in Beirut, Lebanon, 1938
Studied at the Avni School of Fine Arts, Tel Aviv (1959–61); St. Martin's School of Art, London (1966)
Lives in New York

Selected Solo Exhibitions: Mayfair Gallery, London, 1970; Israel Museum, Jerusalem, 1972; Stedelijk Museum, Amsterdam, 1974; Palais des Beaux-Arts, Brussels, 1976; Whitney Museum of American Art, New York, New American Filmmakers Series, 1977.

Selected Group Exhibitions: 6e Biennale de Paris, 1969; Kassel, West Germany, Documenta 6, 1977; Musée National d'Art Moderne, Centre National d'Art et de Culture Georges Pompidou, Paris, 1979; International Cultural Centre, Antwerp, "Beyond Surface," 1980.

Rafael Ferrer

Born in San Juan, Puerto Rico, 1933
Studied at Syracuse University, New York (1951); University of Puerto Rico, Rio Piedras (1952)
Lives in Philadelphia

Selected Solo Exhibitions: University of Puerto Rico, Mayaguez, 1964; Museum of Contemporary Art, Chicago, 1972; Delaware Art Museum, Wilmington, 1974; Albright-Knox Art Gallery, Buffalo, New York, 1977; The New Gallery, Cleveland, 1978; Nancy Hoffman Gallery, New York, 1978; Frumkin/Struve Gallery, Chicago, 1980; Hamilton Gallery of Contemporary Art, New York, 1980.

Selected Group Exhibitions: Martha Jackson Gallery, New York, "Young Artists: Their Work," 1967; Whitney Museum of American Art, New York, "Anti-Illusion: Procedures/Materials," 1969; Whitney Museum of American Art, "Annual Exhibition: Contemporary American Sculpture," 1970; Whitney Museum of American Art, 1973 Biennial Exhibition; Museum of Contemporary Art, Chicago, "A View of a Decade," 1977; Institute of Contemporary Art of The University of Pennsylvania, Philadelphia, "Masks, Tents, Vessels, Talismans," 1979.

Robert Fichter

Born in Fort Meyers, Florida, 1939
Studied at the University of Florida, Gainesville (B.F.A., 1963); Indiana University, Bloomington (M.F.A., 1966)
Lives in Tallahassee, Florida

Selected Solo Exhibitions: University of California, Davis, 1970; Infinite Gallery, Seattle, Washington, 1972; Visual Studies Workshop, Rochester, New York, organizer, 1971 (traveled nationally); Light Gallery, New York, 1974; School of The Art Institute of Chicago, 1974; University of New Mexico, Albuquerque, 1975; Light Gallery, 1976; Robert Freidus Gallery, New York, 1980.

Selected Group Exhibitions: Akron Art Institute, Akron, Ohio, "Into the 70's," 1970; National Gallery of Canada, Ottawa, Ontario, "The Photograph as Object, 1843–1969," 1970; Memorial Union Art Gallery, University of California, Davis, "California Photography 1970," 1970 (traveled nationally); International Museum of Photography at George Eastman House, Rochester, New York, "60's Continuum," 1972; Fogg Art Museum, Harvard University, Cambridge, Massachusetts, "Photography Unlimited," 1974; Los Angeles Institute of Contemporary Art, "Exposing: Photographic Definitions," 1976; Light Gallery, New York, "20 x 24 Polaroid," 1979.

Vernon Fisher

Born in Fort Worth, 1943
Studied at Hardin-Simmons University, Abilene (B.A., 1967); University of Illinois, Champaign-Urbana (M.F.A., 1969)
Lives in Denton, Texas

Fisher *(cont.)*

Selected Solo Exhibitions: North Texas State University, Denton, 1970; Tyler Museum of Art, Tyler, Texas, 1973; Delahunty Gallery, Dallas, 1975; Tyler Museum of Art, 1975; Wichita Falls Museum and Art Center, Texas, 1975; William Sawyer Gallery, San Francisco, 1976; University of Texas, Dallas, 1976; Delahunty Gallery, 1977; Denise René/Hans Mayer, Düsseldorf, West Germany, 1980.

Selected Group Exhibitions: Fort Worth Art Museum, "Project South/ Southwest: Younger American Artists," 1970; Fort Worth Art Museum, "Southwest Tarrant County Annual 1971," 1971; Art Museum of South Texas, Corpus Christi, "Exhibition of Ten Texas Painters," 1972; Fort Worth Art Museum, "Southwest Tarrant County Annual 1973," 1973; Fort Worth Art Museum, "Southwest Tarrant County Annual 1975," 1975; Fort Worth Art Museum, "Exchange DFW/SFO," 1975 (traveled nationally); Fort Worth Art Museum, "Southwest Tarrant County Annual 1977," 1977; Contemporary Arts Museum, Houston, "American Narrative/Story Art, 1967–1977," 1977 (traveled nationally); Contemporary Arts Museum, Houston, "Fire," 1979; University Art Museum, University of Texas, Austin, "Made in Texas," 1979; The New Museum, New York, "Investigation: Probe—Structure—Analysis," 1980.

Kit Fitzgerald and John Sanborn

Kit Fitzgerald
Born in Springfield, Massachusetts, 1953
Studied at Smith College, Northhampton, Massachusetts
Lives in New York

John Sanborn
Born in Copiague, New York, 1954
Studied at New York University
Lives in New York

Selected Solo Exhibitions: Three Mercer Street Store, New York, 1976; Museum of Fine Arts, Boston, 1978; The Museum of Modern Art, New York, 1978; The Kitchen Center for Video, Music and Dance, New York, 1978; Whitney Museum of American Art, New York, New American Filmmakers Series, 1979; University Art Museum, University of California, Berkeley, 1979; San Francisco Art Institute Galleries, 1979; Cirque Divers, Liège, Belgium, 1980; Acme Gallery, London, 1980; The Kitchen Center for Video, Music and Dance, 1980; American Center, Paris, 1980.

Selected Group Exhibitions: Whitney Museum of American Art, New York, 1979 Biennial Exhibition; Museum of Contemporary Art, Chicago, "Video: The Electronic Medium," 1980; Musée d'Art Moderne de la Ville de Paris, "New American Video," 1980; San Francisco Video Festival, "Video 80," 1980; The Art Museum, Princeton University, Princeton, New Jersey, "Video-Television," 1980; Art Gallery of Ontario, Toronto, "Projected Parts," 1980.

Richard Fleischner

Born in New York, 1944
Studied at the Rhode Island School of Design, Providence (B.F.A., 1966; M.F.A., 1968)
Lives in Providence, Rhode Island

Selected Solo Exhibitions and Installations: Terry Dintenfass Gallery, New York, 1971; Hopkins Art Center, Dartmouth College, Hanover, New Hampshire, 1971; Terry Dintenfass Gallery, 1973, 1975; Artpark, Lewiston, New York, *Wood Interior*, 1976 (site installation); Hammarskjold Plaza, New York, *Sod Construction*, 1976 (site installation); University Gallery, University of Massachusetts, Amherst, 1977; Woodlawn, Maryland, *The Baltimore Project*, 1978–80 (site installation); Dayton, Ohio, *Dayton Project*, 1978 (site installation); Museum of Art, Rhode Island School of Design, Providence, 1980; Max Protetch Gallery, New York, 1980.

Selected Group Exhibitions and Installations: Madison Art Center, Madison, Wisconsin, "Small Environments," 1972; Newport, Rhode Island,

"Monumenta," *Sod Maze,* 1974 (site installation); Far Hills, New Jersey, "Projects in Nature," *Sod Drawing,* 1975 (site installation); Wheaton College, Norton, Massachusetts, "Labyrinths," 1975; Greenwich, Connecticut, "Sculpture '76," *Sod Drawing,* 1976 (site installation); Kassel, West Germany, Documenta 6, 1977; Protetch-McIntosh Gallery, Washington, D.C., "Art and Architecture, Space and Structure," 1979; XIII Winter Olympic Games, Lake Placid, New York, "Environmental Art," *Fence/Covered Fence,* 1979–80 (site installation); Los Angeles Institute of Contemporary Art, "Architectural Sculpture," 1980; 39th Venice Biennale, 1980; Institute of Contemporary Art of The University of Pennsylvania, Philadelphia, "Drawings: The Pluralist Decade," 1980.

Hollis Frampton

Born in Wooster, Ohio, 1936
Studied at Case Western Reserve University, Cleveland (1954–57)
Lives in Eaton, New York

SELECTED SOLO EXHIBITIONS: Filmmakers Cinematheque, New York, 1966, 1969, 1970; The Museum of Modern Art, New York, 1970; Canyon Cinematheque, San Francisco, 1971; Musée d'Art Moderne de la Ville de Paris, 1971; Museum of Contemporary Art, Chicago, 1972; Walker Art Center, Minneapolis, 1972; Pacific Film Archive, University Art Museum, Berkeley, California, 1972; The Museum of Modern Art, New York, 1973; Anthology Film Archives, New York, 1975; Whitney Museum of American Art, New York, New American Filmmakers Series, 1976, 1980.

SELECTED GROUP EXHIBITIONS: Toronto Cinethon, Ontario, 1967; The Museum of Modern Art, New York, "Information," 1970; Whitney Museum of American Art, New York, New American Filmmakers Series, "New Cinema," 1971; The Solomon R. Guggenheim Museum, New York, "New Forms in Film," 1972; Vancouver Art Gallery, Vancouver, British Columbia, "Form and Structure in Recent Film," 1972; Whitney Museum of American Art, "Five Expansions in Visions," 1973; Whitney Museum of American Art, 1979 Biennial Exhibition.

Richard Francisco

Born in St. Helena, California, 1942
Lives in New York

SELECTED SOLO EXHIBITIONS: Betty Parsons Gallery, New York, 1973; Daniel Weinberg Gallery, San Francisco, 1974; Henie-Onstad Art Center, Oslo, Norway, 1974; Gentofte Kunstbibliotek, Denmark, 1974–75 (traveled internationally); Galleria dell'Ariete, Milan, 1975; Betty Parsons Gallery, 1975, 1977, 1978; Galleria Bonomo, Bari, Italy, 1978; Betty Parsons Gallery, 1979; Stedelijk Museum, Amsterdam, 1980; Linda Farris Gallery, Seattle, Washington, 1980.

SELECTED GROUP EXHIBITIONS: California State University, Los Angeles, "New Work/New York," 1976; Whitney Museum of American Art, New York, Downtown Branch, "Small Objects," 1977; International Cultural Centre, Antwerp, 1980.

Robert Frank

Born in Zurich, 1924
Lives in Nova Scotia

SELECTED SOLO EXHIBITIONS: New York Theater, New York, 1969; Kunsthaus Zürich, 1976; Yajima Galerie, Montreal, 1977; The Photo Gallery of the National Film Board of Canada, Ottawa, 1978; Whitney Museum of American Art, New York, New American Filmmakers Series, 1980.

SELECTED GROUP EXHIBITIONS: The Museum of Modern Art, New York, 1948, 1949, 1952, 1954; The Art Institute of Chicago, 1955; International Museum of Photography at George Eastman House, Rochester, New York, 1955; The Museum of Modern Art, New York, 1962; San Francisco Museum of Art, 1967; Whitney Museum of American Art, New York, New American Filmmakers Series, "In the Family," 1971; Cleveland Museum of Art, 1978.

Howard Fried

Born in Cleveland, 1946
Studied at the San Francisco Art Institute (B.F.A., 1968); University of California, Davis (M.F.A., 1970)
Lives in San Francisco

SELECTED SOLO EXHIBITIONS: Reese Palley Gallery, New York, 1971; San Francisco Art Institute, 1972; Nova Scotia College of Art and Design, Halifax, 1972; San Francisco Museum of Modern Art, 1977; Everson Museum of Art, Syracuse, New York, 1978; Fort Worth Art Museum, 1979; The Museum of Modern Art, New York, 1979.

SELECTED GROUP EXHIBITIONS: Kunstmuseum Düsseldorf, West Germany, "Prospect 71—Projections," 1971; Kassel, West Germany, Documenta 5, 1972; Wallraf-Richartz Museum, Cologne, West Germany, "Projekt 74—Stadt Köln," 1974; Independent Curators Associates, Washington, D.C., organizer, "From Self-Portrait to Autobiographical Art," 1978–79 (traveled nationally); San Francisco Museum of Modern Art, "Space/Time/Sound—1970's: A Decade in the Bay Area," 1979; Whitney Museum of American Art, New York, New American Filmmakers Series, "Boord/Fried/Froese," 1979; Whitney Museum of American Art, 1979 Biennial Exhibition.

Benno Friedman

Born in New York, 1945
Studied at Brandeis University, Waltham, Massachusetts (B.A., 1966)
Lives in New York

SELECTED SOLO EXHIBITIONS: Underground Gallery, New York, 1969; Light Gallery, New York, 1973; Tucson Museum of Art, Arizona, 1973; Light Gallery, 1975, 1976, 1977; Atlantic Richfield Company (ARCO) Center for Visual Art, Los Angeles, 1978; Light Gallery, 1978; Asher-Faure Gallery, Los Angeles, 1980.

SELECTED GROUP EXHIBITIONS: Hayden Gallery, Massachusetts Institute of Technology, Cambridge, "Being Without Clothes," 1971; International Museum of Photography at George Eastman House, Rochester, New York, "60's Continuum," 1972; Hayden Gallery, "Octave of Prayer," 1972; Vassar College Art Gallery, Poughkeepsie, New York, "New Art from Photo-sensitized Materials," 1972; The Hudson River Museum, Yonkers, New York, "Light and Lens: Methods of Photography," 1973; Museum of Fine Arts, Boston, "Private Realities," 1974; Herbert F. Johnson Museum of Art, Cornell University, Ithaca, New York, "Photo/Synthesis," 1976; International Center for Photography, New York, "Masters of the Camera: Stieglitz, Steichen and Their Successors," 1976 (traveled internationally); Philadelphia College of Art, "The Hand Colored Photograph," 1979; International Museum of Photography at George Eastman House, "The Photographer's Hand," 1979.

Jedd Garet

Born in Los Angeles, 1955
Studied at the Rhode Island School of Design, Providence (1975–76); School of Visual Arts, New York (B.F.A., 1977)
Lives in New York

SELECTED SOLO EXHIBITIONS: Felicity Samuel Gallery, London, 1979; Robert Miller Gallery, New York, 1979; Galerie Bischofsberger, Zurich, 1980.

SELECTED GROUP EXHIBITIONS: Hans Strelow Gallery, Düsseldorf, West Germany, "Young Americans of the Eighties," 1980; Whitney Museum of American Art, New York, Downtown Branch, "Painting in Relief," 1980; Barbara Gladstone Gallery, New York, "Interiors," 1980; 39th Venice Biennale, 1980.

Ernie Gehr

Born in 1943
Lives in New York

SELECTED SOLO EXHIBITIONS: Rocky Mountain Film Center, Colorado, 1979;

Collective for Living Cinema, New York, 1979; Millennium Film Workshop, New York, 1979; The Museum of Modern Art, New York, 1979; Walker Art Center, Minneapolis, 1980.

Barry Gerson

Born in Philadelphia, 1939
Lives in New York

SELECTED SOLO EXHIBITIONS: Whitney Museum of American Art, New York, New American Filmmakers Series, 1976, 1977; The Museum of Modern Art, New York, 1977; Albright-Knox Art Gallery, Buffalo, New York, 1978.

SELECTED GROUP EXHIBITIONS: Montreux, Switzerland, "New Forms in Film," 1974; Whitney Museum of American Art, New York, New American Filmmakers Series, "Luminous Zone," 1974; Museum of Contemporary Art, Chicago, "A History of the American Avant-Garde Cinema," 1977; Moderna Museet, Stockholm, "The Pleasure Dome: American Experimental Film," 1980.

Davidson Gigliotti

Born in Winchester, Massachusetts, 1939
Studied at the Rhode Island School of Design, Providence (1957–59); Hartford Art School of the University of Hartford, West Hartford, Connecticut (1959); School of The Art Institute of Chicago (1960); New York University (1962–64)
Lives in New York

SELECTED SOLO EXHIBITIONS: The Kitchen Center for Video, Music and Dance, New York, 1974, 1975; Anthology Film Archives, New York, 1975; Jamaica Art Center, New York, 1977; The Museum of Modern Art, New York, 1979; P.S. 1, Institute for Art and Urban Resources, Long Island City, New York, 1980; Everson Museum of Art, Syracuse, New York, 1980.

SELECTED GROUP EXHIBITIONS: Firehouse Gallery, Nassau Community College, Garden City, New York, "Video Vis A Tergo," 1980; Lenbachhaus, Munich, West Germany, "New York Video," 1980; P.S. 1, Institute for Art and Urban Resources, Long Island City, New York, "Landscape Video," 1980.

Frank Gillette

Born in Jersey City, New Jersey, 1941
Studied at Pratt Institute, Brooklyn, New York (1959–62)
Lives in New York

SELECTED SOLO EXHIBITIONS: Everson Museum of Art, Syracuse, New York, 1973; Art-Tapes 22, Florence, 1974; The Kitchen Center for Video, Music and Dance, New York, 1974; Long Beach Museum of Art, California, 1975; Anthology Film Archives, New York, 1975; Leo Castelli Gallery, New York, 1977; Whitney Museum of American Art, New York, New American Filmmakers Series, 1977; Contemporary Arts Museum, Houston, 1978; Robinson Gallery, Houston, 1978; Honolulu Academy of Arts, 1979; University Art Museum, University of California, Berkeley, 1979; Corcoran Gallery of Art, Washington, D.C., 1980.

SELECTED GROUP EXHIBITIONS: Howard Wise Gallery, New York, "T.V. as a Creative Medium," 1969; Kunsthalle, Cologne, West Germany, "Project-74," 1974; Leo Castelli Gallery, New York, 1976; Sonnabend Gallery, New York, 1976; Kassel, West Germany, Documenta 6, 1977; P.S. 1, Institute for Art and Urban Resources, Long Island City, New York, "Landscape Video," 1980.

Bette Gordon

Born in Boston, 1950
Studied at the University of Wisconsin, Madison (B.A., 1968; M.A., 1975; M.F.A., 1976); La Sorbonne (Ie Degré de la Langue et la Littérature, 1971)
Lives in New York

SELECTED SOLO EXHIBITIONS: Millennium Film Workshop, New York, 1976; Walker Art Center, Minneapolis, 1977; Chicago Filmmakers, 1977; Collective for

Gordon *(cont.)*

Living Cinema, New York, 1977; Institute of Contemporary Art, Boston, 1978; Media Study, Buffalo, New York, 1980; Chicago Filmmakers, 1980; Collective for Living Cinema, 1980.

SELECTED GROUP EXHIBITIONS: Whitney Museum of American Art, New York, New American Filmmakers Series, "Stills," 1975; Edinburgh International Film Festival, 1978, 1979; The Kitchen Center for Video, Music and Dance, New York, "Filmworks," 1979; Third International Avant-Garde Film Festival, London, 1979; Festival International de Jeune Cinéma, Hyères, France, 1980.

Shalom Gorewitz

Born in New York, 1949
Studied at Antioch College, Valencia, California (1960–64); California Institute of the Arts, Valencia (B.F.A., 1971)
Lives in New York

SELECTED SOLO EXHIBITIONS: New York City Cable Television, 1978; Hal Bromm Gallery, New York, 1979; The Museum of Modern Art, New York, 1979; Media Study, Buffalo, New York, 1980; Anthology Film Archives, New York, 1980; WTTW, Chicago, 1980.

SELECTED GROUP EXHIBITIONS: The Kitchen Center for Video, Music and Dance, New York, "Image Processing," 1979, 1980; San Francisco Video Festival, "Video 80," 1980; Athens Video Festival, Athens, Ohio, 1980; The Kitchen Center for Video, Music and Dance, "Videotapes from the Kitchen Center for Video and Music," 1980 (traveled internationally).

Larry Gottheim

Born in New York, 1936
Studied at Oberlin College, Oberlin, Ohio (B.A., 1957); Yale University, New Haven, Connecticut (Ph.D., 1965)
Lives in Binghamton, New York

SELECTED SOLO EXHIBITIONS: Millennium Film Workshop, New York, 1972; Collective for Living Cinema, New York, 1973; The Museum of Modern Art, New York, 1974; Whitney Museum of American Art, New York, New American Filmmakers Series, 1974; Museum of Art, Carnegie Institute, Pittsburgh, 1975; Whitney Museum of American Art, New American Filmmakers Series, 1976; San Francisco Museum of Modern Art, 1976; Collective for Living Cinema, 1976; Anthology Film Archives, New York, 1976; The Museum of Modern Art, New York, 1978; Whitney Museum of American Art, New American Filmmakers Series, 1978; University of Hawaii, Honolulu, 1980.

SELECTED GROUP EXHIBITIONS: Hamburg Filmschau, West Germany, 1973; National Film Theater, London, "Festival of Independent Avant-Garde Film," 1973; Whitney Museum of American Art, New York, 1979 Biennial Exhibition; Moderna Museet, Stockholm, "The Pleasure Dome: American Experimental Film," 1980; Berlin Film Festival, 1980; Collective for Living Cinema, New York, "North American Landscapes," 1980.

Jan Groover

Born in Plainfield, New Jersey, 1943
Studied at Pratt Institute, Brooklyn, New York (B.F.A., 1965); Ohio State University, Columbus (M.F.A., 1970)
Lives in New York

SELECTED SOLO EXHIBITIONS: Light Gallery, New York, 1974; Max Protetch Gallery, New York, 1976; Corcoran Gallery of Art, Washington, D.C., 1976; International Museum of Photography at George Eastman House, Rochester, New York, 1976; Sonnabend Gallery, New York, 1977; The Baltimore Museum of Art, 1977; Sonnabend Gallery, 1978.

SELECTED GROUP EXHIBITIONS: Lowe Art Museum, University of Miami, Coral Gables, Florida, "Time and Transformation," 1975; San Francisco Museum of

Modern Art, "New Directions in Color Photography," 1976; The Museum of Fine Arts, Houston, "Contemporary American Photographic Works," 1977 (traveled nationally); Whitney Museum of American Art, New York, "Jan Groover/David Haxton," 1978; The Museum of Modern Art, New York, "Mirrors and Windows: American Photography Since 1960," 1978.

Duane Hanson

Born in Alexandria, Minnesota, 1925
Studied at Luther College, Decorah, Iowa (1943); University of Washington, Seattle (1944); Macalester College, St. Paul, Minnesota (B.A., 1946); University of Minnesota, Minneapolis (1947); Cranbrook Academy of Art, Bloomfield Hills, Michigan (M.F.A., 1951)
Lives in Davie, Florida

Selected Solo Exhibitions: Cranbrook Academy of Art/Museum, Bloomfield Hills, Michigan, 1951; Galerie Netzel, Bremen, West Germany, 1958; O.K. Harris Gallery, New York, 1970, 1972; Museum of Contemporary Art, Chicago, 1974; Edwin A. Ulrich Museum of Art, Wichita State University, Kansas, 1976 (traveled nationally); O.K. Harris Gallery, 1980.

Selected Group Exhibitions: Walker Art Center, Minneapolis, 1946; Whitney Museum of American Art, New York, "Human Concern/Personal Torment: The Grotesque in American Art," 1968; Whitney Museum of American Art, "Annual Exhibition: Contemporary American Sculpture," 1970; Museum of Contemporary Art, Chicago, "Radical Realism," 1971; Kassel, West Germany, Documenta 5, 1972; The Art Institute of Chicago, "Seventy-first American Exhibition," 1974; The Denver Art Museum, "Reality of Illusion," 1979–80 (traveled nationally); Whitney Museum of American Art, "The Figurative Tradition and the Whitney Museum of American Art," 1980.

Martha Haslanger

Born in Dearborn, Michigan, 1947
Lives in New York

Selected Solo Exhibitions: London Filmmakers Cooperative, 1977; Berlin Forum/Arsenal, West Germany, 1977; Stadtmuseum, Munich, West Germany, 1977; Hamburg Filmgroup, West Germany, 1977; Chicago Filmgroup, 1977; Collective for Living Cinema, New York, 1977; Boston Film/Video Foundation, 1978; Millennium Film Workshop, New York, 1978; Collective for Living Cinema, 1979; Independent Film Oasis of Los Angeles, 1979; Philadelphia College of Art, 1979; London Filmmakers Cooperative, 1979; Media Study, Buffalo, New York, 1980; Independent Film Oasis of Los Angeles, 1980; Boston Film/Video Foundation, 1980.

Selected Group Exhibitions: Fifth Annual Film Competition, Knokke-Heist, Belgium, "EXPRMNTL-5," 1975; Whitney Museum of American Art, New York, New American Filmmakers Series, "Text and Image: Davidovich/Haslanger/Myers," 1976; Third International Avant-Garde Festival, London, 1979; Whitney Museum of American Art, 1979 Biennial Exhibition; Festival du Jeune Cinéma, Hyères, France, 1980; Arts Council of Great Britain, London, "Film as Film," 1980–82 (traveling internationally).

David Haxton

Born in Indianapolis, Indiana, 1943
Studied at the University of South Florida, Tampa (B.A., 1965); University of Michigan, Ann Arbor (M.F.A., 1967)
Lives in New York

Selected Solo Exhibitions: Anthology Film Archives, New York, 1976 (films); Sonnabend Gallery, New York, 1977 (films); Anthology Film Archives, 1978 (films); The Museum of Modern Art, New York, 1978 (films); Sonnabend Gallery, 1979, 1980; CEPA, Photo Workshop and Gallery, Buffalo, New York, 1980.

Selected Group Exhibitions: Sonnabend Gallery, New York, "Films by Artists," 1974; Whitney Museum of American Art, New York, New American Filmmakers

Haxton *(cont.)*

Series, "Space and Time," 1975; Thomas Segal Gallery, Boston, "Color Photographs," 1978; Whitney Museum of American Art, "David Haxton/Jan Groover," 1978; Artists Space, New York, "Artists Films," 1978; The Museum of Modern Art, New York, "Selections from the Permanent Collection," 1979; Palazzo Grazzi, Venice, "The Art of Performance," 1979; Williams College Museum of Art, Williamstown, Massachusetts, "Six Photographers: Six Unconventional Views," 1979; Santa Barbara Museum of Art, "American Photography in the 1970's," 1979; Light Gallery, New York, "One of a Kind," 1979 (traveled nationally); Whitney Museum of American Art, 1979 Biennial Exhibition; The Clocktower, Institute for Art and Urban Resources, New York, "Film as Installation," 1980; Art Museum, University of California, Santa Barbara, "Invented Images," 1980 (traveled nationally); Art Gallery, University of California, Irvine, "Situational Imagery," 1980.

Al Held

Born in New York, 1928
Studied at The Art Students League of New York (1948–49); Académie de la Grande Chaumière, Paris
Lives in New York and Boiceville, New York

Selected Solo Exhibitions: Galerie Huit, Paris, 1952; Poindexter Gallery, New York, 1959, 1960, 1961, 1962; André Emmerich Gallery, New York, 1965; Stedelijk Museum, Amsterdam, 1966; Institute of Contemporary Art of The University of Pennsylvania, Philadelphia, 1968; San Francisco Museum of Art, 1968; Corcoran Gallery of Art, Washington, D.C., 1968; Whitney Museum of American Art, New York, 1974; Museum of Contemporary Art, Boston, 1978; André Emmerich Gallery, 1980.

Selected Group Exhibitions: Tanager Gallery, New York, 1955; Spoleto, Italy, "Festival of Two Worlds," 1958; Whitney Museum of American Art, New York, "Geometric Abstraction in America," 1962, "Annual Exhibition: Contemporary American Sculpture," 1964; Los Angeles County Museum of Art, "Post-Painterly Abstraction," 1964 (traveled nationally); Whitney Museum of American Art, "Annual Exhibition: Contemporary American Painting," 1965, 1967; The Art Institute of Chicago, "29th Exhibition by the Society for Contemporary Art," 1969; Whitney Museum of American Art, "Annual Exhibition: Contemporary American Painting," 1969, 1972; Whitney Museum of American Art, 1973 Biennial Exhibition; Corcoran Gallery of Art, Washington, D.C., 34th Biennial of Contemporary American Painting, 1975; Museum of Contemporary Art, Chicago, "A View of a Decade," 1977; Anderson Gallery, Virginia Commonwealth University, Richmond, "Late Twentieth Century Art: The Sydney and Frances Lewis Foundation," 1979 (traveled nationally); Museum of Fine Arts, Montgomery, Alabama, "Art Inc.: American Paintings from Corporate Collections," 1979 (traveled nationally).

Nancy Holt

Born in Worcester, Massachusetts, 1938
Studied at Jackson College, Tufts University, Medford, Massachusetts (B.S., 1960)
Lives in New York

Selected Solo Exhibitions: University of Montana, Missoula, 1972; University of Rhode Island, Kingston, 1972; LoGiudice Gallery, New York, 1973; Bykert Gallery, New York, 1974; Walter Kelly Gallery, Chicago, 1974; Franklin Furnace, New York, 1977; John Weber Gallery, New York, 1979; Art Museum, Miami University, Oxford, Ohio, 1979.

Selected Group Exhibitions: Artpark, Lewiston, New York, *Hydra's Head*, 1974 (site installation); Whitney Museum of American Art, New York, 1977 Biennial Exhibition, 1979 Biennial Exhibition; The Wellesley College Museum, Wellesley, Massachusetts, "Site Work: Aspects of the Seventies," 1980; Los Angeles Institute of Contemporary Art, "Architectural Sculpture," 1980; Hampshire College Gallery, Amherst, Massachusetts, "A Sense of Place: The American Landscape in Recent Art," 1980.

Bryan Hunt

Born in Terre Haute, Indiana, 1947
Studied at the University of South Florida, Tampa (1966–68); Otis Art Institute, Los Angeles (B.F.A., 1971); Whitney Museum of American Art Independent Study Program, New York (1972)
Lives in New York

SELECTED SOLO EXHIBITIONS: The Clocktower, Institute of Art and Urban Resources, New York, 1974; Jack Glenn Gallery, Corona del Mar, California, 1974; Daniel Weinberg Gallery, San Francisco, 1976; Blum/Helman Gallery, New York, 1977, 1978; Daniel Weinberg Gallery, 1978; Greenberg Gallery, St. Louis, Missouri, 1978; Blum/Helman Gallery, 1979; Bernard Jacobson Gallery, London, 1979; Blum/Helman Gallery, 1979; Galerie Bruno Bischofsberger, Zurich, 1979; Margo Leavin Gallery, Los Angeles, 1980.

SELECTED GROUP EXHIBITIONS: The Solomon R. Guggenheim Museum, New York, "Young American Artist," 1978; Stedelijk Museum, Amsterdam, "Made by Sculptors," 1978; Whitney Museum of American Art, New York, 1979 Biennial Exhibition; University Gallery, University of Massachusetts, Amherst, "Sculpture on the Wall—Relief Sculpture of the 70s," 1980; 39th Venice Biennale, 1980.

Taka Iimura

Born in Tokyo, 1937
Studied at Keio University, Tokyo (B.A., 1959)
Lives in New York

SELECTED SOLO EXHIBITIONS: Naiqua Gallery, Tokyo, 1963; Filmmakers Cinematheque, New York, 1966; Swedish Film Institute, Stockholm, 1969; Japan House, New York, 1972; The Museum of Modern Art, New York, 1975; Art Gallery of Ontario, Toronto, 1978; Centre National d'Art et de Culture Georges Pompidou, Paris, 1979; Whitney Museum of American Art, New York, New American Filmmakers Series, 1979; Studio 200, Tokyo, 1980.

SELECTED GROUP EXHIBITIONS: Third International Experimental Film Festival, Brussels, 1963; The Museum of Modern Art, New York, "Japanese Experimental Films," 1966; Everson Museum of Art, Syracuse, New York, "Circuit," 1973; Institute of Contemporary Art of The University of Pennsylvania, Philadelphia, "Video Art," 1976; Sogetsu Hall, Tokyo, "International Video Art," 1978.

Ken Jacobs

Born in New York, 1933
Lives in New York

SELECTED SOLO EXHIBITIONS *(Theater Works):* Anthology Film Archives, New York, 1975; Collective for Living Cinema, New York, 1975, 1976; Beat Theater, Rome, 1977; Entermedia Theater, New York, 1977; Collective for Living Cinema, 1977; Whitney Museum of American Art, New York, New American Filmmakers Series, 1979; Minneapolis College of Design, 1979; McGill University, Montreal, 1980; Cinéma Parallele, Montreal, 1980; Boston Film/Video Foundation, 1980; Collective for Living Cinema, 1980.

SELECTED GROUP EXHIBITIONS *(Theater Works):* London Film Festival, 1973; Gallery Ariadne, New York, "Binocular Works," 1975; Whitney Museum of American Art, New York, New American Filmmakers Series, 1975; Kassel, West Germany, Documenta 6, 1977.

Neil Jenney

Born in Torrington, Connecticut, 1945
Self-taught
Lives in New York

SELECTED SOLO EXHIBITIONS: Rudolf Zwirner Gallery, Cologne, West Germany, 1968; Noah Goldowsky Gallery, New York, 1970; David Whitney Gallery, New York, 1970; Blum/Helman Gallery, New York, 1975; Wadsworth Atheneum, Hartford, Connecticut, 1976.

Jenney *(cont.)*

Selected Group Exhibitions: Richard Bellamy/Noah Goldowsky Gallery, New York, "Arp to Artschwager II," 1967; The Detroit Institute of Arts, "Other Ideas," 1969; Whitney Museum of American Art, New York, "Anti-Illusion: Procedures/ Materials," 1969; Whitney Museum of American Art, "Annual Exhibition: Contemporary American Painting," 1969; Allen Memorial Art Museum, Oberlin College, Oberlin, Ohio, "Three American Artists: C. Close, R. Cooper, N. Jenney," 1970; Kassel, West Germany, Documenta 5, 1972; Whitney Museum of American Art, 1973 Biennial Exhibition; The Museum of Modern Art, New York, "76 Jefferson Street," 1975; The Metropolitan Museum of Art, New York and The Fine Arts Museums of San Francisco, organizers, "Representations of America," 1977 (traveled in the Soviet Union); The New Museum, New York, "Bad Painting," 1978; Whitney Museum of American Art, "New Image Painting," 1978.

Bill Jensen

Born in Minneapolis, 1945
Studied at the University of Minnesota, Minneapolis (B.F.A., 1968; M.F.A., 1970)
Lives in New York

Selected Solo Exhibitions: Fischbach Gallery, New York, 1973; The Gallery of July and August, Woodstock, New York, 1974; Fischbach Gallery, 1975; Washburn Gallery, New York, 1980.

Selected Group Exhibitions: Lowe Art Gallery, Syracuse University, Syracuse, New York, "Contemporary Painting," 1976; P.S. 1, Institute for Art and Urban Resources, Long Island City, New York, "Rooms," 1976; The New Museum, New York, "Double Take," 1978; Grey Art Gallery, New York University, "American Painting; The Eighties," 1979 (traveled internationally); The New Museum, "The 1970s: New American Painting," 1979 (traveled internationally); Neuberger Museum, State University of New York, College at Purchase, "Seven Artists," 1980.

Steve Keister

Born in Lancaster, Pennsylvania, 1949
Studied at Tyler School of Art, Temple University, Philadelphia (B.F.A., 1970; M.F.A., 1972)
Lives in New York

Selected Solo Exhibitions: Nancy Lurie Gallery, Chicago, 1977; Pam Adler Gallery, New York, 1978; Nancy Lurie Gallery, 1979; Texas Gallery, Houston, 1980; Museum of Contemporary Art, Chicago, 1980.

Selected Group Exhibitions: P.S. 1, Institute for Art and Urban Resources, Long Island City, New York, "Special Projects," 1978; The New Museum, New York, "New Work/New York," 1978; Albright-Knox Art Gallery, Buffalo, New York, "Eight Sculptors," 1979; Texas Gallery, Houston, "N.Y.TEOWZ," 1980.

Ellsworth Kelly

Born in Newburgh, New York, 1923
Studied at Pratt Institute, Brooklyn, New York (1941–42); School of the Museum of Fine Arts, Boston (1946–48)
Lives in Chatham, New York

Selected Solo Exhibitions: Galerie Arnaud, Paris, 1951; Betty Parsons Gallery, New York, 1956, 1957, 1959, 1961, 1963; Washington Gallery of Modern Art, Washington, D.C., 1963–64 (traveled nationally); Galerie Maeght, Paris, 1964; Sidney Janis Gallery, New York, 1968; The Museum of Modern Art, New York, 1973 (traveled nationally); Leo Castelli Gallery, New York, 1977; The Metropolitan Museum of Art, New York, 1979; Stedelijk Museum, Amsterdam, 1979–80 (traveled internationally).

Selected Group Exhibitions: Boris Mirski Art Gallery, Boston, 1948; Galerie Beaux-Arts, Paris, "Premier Salon des Jeunes Peintres," 1950; Whitney Museum of American Art, New York, "Young America, 1957," 1957; Whitney Museum of American Art, "Annual Exhibition: Contemporary American Painting," 1959; Los Angeles County Museum of Art, "Post-Painterly Abstraction," 1964 (traveled internationally); The Solomon R. Guggenheim Museum, New York, "Systemic Painting," 1966; Whitney Museum of American Art, "Annual Exhibition: Contemporary American Painting," 1967; Institute of Contemporary Art of The University of Pennsylvania, Philadelphia, "Grids," 1972; The Solomon R. Guggenheim Museum, "Twentieth Century American Drawing: Three Avant-Garde Generations," 1976 (traveled internationally); Corcoran Gallery of Art, Washington, D.C., "36th Biennial Exhibition of Contemporary American Painting," 1979; Whitney Museum of American Art, 1979 Biennial Exhibition.

Edward Kienholz

Born in Fairfield, Washington, 1927
Studied at Eastern Washington State College, Cheney, Washington; Whitworth College, Spokane, Washington; and other western colleges
Lives in Hope, Idaho, and West Berlin

Selected Solo Exhibitions: Cafe Galleria, Los Angeles, 1955; Ferus Gallery, Los Angeles, 1958, 1960, 1961; Pasadena Art Museum, California, 1961; Ferus Gallery, 1963; Alexander Iolas Gallery, New York, 1963; Barney's Beanery, Los Angeles, 1965; Dwan Gallery, Los Angeles and New York, 1965; Los Angeles County Museum of Art, 1966; Institute of Contemporary Art, Boston, 1966; Louisiana Museum, Humlebaek, Denmark, 1979 (traveled internationally).

Selected Group Exhibitions: Los Angeles County Museum of Art, "Sculpture of the Sixties," 1967; The Museum of Modern Art, New York, "Dada, Surrealism and Their Heritage," 1968; Whitney Museum of American Art, New York, "Human Concern/Personal Torment: The Grotesque in American Art," 1969; Kassel, West Germany, Documenta 5, 1972; 37th Venice Biennale, 1976.

Robert Kushner

Born in Pasadena, California, 1949
Studied at the University of California, San Diego (B.A., 1970)
Lives in New York

Selected Solo Exhibitions: Holly Solomon Gallery, New York, 1976; Philadelphia College of Art, 1977; Holly Solomon Gallery, 1977; Mayor Gallery, London, 1978; Daniel Templon, Paris, 1979; Holly Solomon Gallery, 1979; Dart Gallery, Chicago, 1980.

Selected Group Exhibitions: Whitney Museum of American Art, New York, 1975 Biennial Exhibition; The Museum of the American Foundation for the Arts, Miami, Florida, "Patterning and Decoration," 1977; P.S. 1, Institute for Art and Urban Resources, Long Island City, New York, "Pattern Painting," 1977; Contemporary Arts Center, Cincinnati, "Arabesque," 1978; Institute of Contemporary Art of The University of Pennsylvania, Philadelphia, "Material Pleasures: The Fabric Workshop at the Institute of Contemporary Art," 1979; Institute of Contemporary Art of The University of Pennsylvania, "The Decorative Impulse," 1979 (traveled nationally); Mannheimer Kunstverein, West Germany, "Dekor," 1980 (traveled internationally); Neue Galerie-Sammlung Ludwig, Aachen, West Germany, "Les Nouveaux Fauves—Die Neuen Wilden," 1980; 39th Venice Biennale, 1980; Contemporary Arts Center, Cincinnati, "From Performances: Costumes and Other Works," 1980; Institute of Contemporary Art of The University of Pennsylvania, "Drawings: The Pluralist Decade," 1980.

Selected Performances: The Kitchen Center for Video, Music and Dance, New York, "The Persian Line," 1975; Holly Solomon Gallery, New York, "Layers," 1978 (traveled internationally); The Museum of Modern Art, New York, "The New York Hat Line," 1978; Los Angeles Institute of Contemporary Art, "Sentimental Fables," 1979.

George Landow

Born in New Haven, Connecticut, 1944
Studied at Pratt Institute, Brooklyn, New York (1963–65)
Lives in Chicago

Landow *(cont.)*

SELECTED SOLO EXHIBITIONS: Museum of Contemporary Art, Chicago, 1970; Museum of Art, Carnegie Institute, Pittsburgh, 1972; Walker Art Center, Minneapolis, 1975; The Museum of Modern Art, New York, 1975; Whitney Museum of American Art, New York, New American Filmmakers Series, 1976; Pasadena Film Forum, California, 1977; Cochise Fine Arts Gallery, Bisbee, Arizona, 1978; California State University, Sacramento, 1980; Collective for Living Cinema, New York, 1980.

SELECTED GROUP EXHIBITIONS: Oesterreichisches Filmmuseum, Vienna, "New American Cinema," 1967; Amsterdam, 16th Fluxus Film Festival, 1967; New York Film Festival, 1969; New Haven, Connecticut, Fourth Yale Film Festival, 1972; Los Angeles International Film Exposition, 1976; Edinburgh International Film Festival, 1979; Moderna Museet, Stockholm, "The Pleasure Dome: American Experimental Film," 1980.

William Larson

Born in Tonawanda, New York, 1942
Studied at the University of Siena, Italy (1963); State University of New York, Buffalo (B.S., 1964); Institute of Design, Illinois Institute of Technology, Chicago (M.S., 1967)
Lives in Wyncote, Pennsylvania

SELECTED SOLO EXHIBITIONS: Maryland Art Institute, Baltimore, 1970; Light Gallery, New York, 1973, 1975; The Art Institute of Chicago, 1977; Light Gallery, 1977, 1978, 1979; Los Angeles Institute of Contemporary Art, 1980.

SELECTED GROUP EXHIBITIONS: University of Exeter, England, "American Contemporary Photography," 1970; San Francisco Art Institute, "Sequence," 1972; Philadelphia Museum of Art, "The Expanded Photograph," 1972; The Hudson River Museum, Yonkers, New York, "Light and Lens," 1973; Akron Art Institute, Akron, Ohio, "Images: Dimensional, Movable, Transferable," 1973; Museum of Art, Rhode Island School of Design, Providence, "Spaces," 1978; Hayden Gallery, Massachusetts Institute of Technology, Cambridge, "American Color Photography," 1978; The Museum of Modern Art, New York, "Mirrors and Windows: American Photography Since 1960," 1978; Everson Museum of Art, Syracuse, New York, "Alternative Imaging Systems," 1979; Santa Barbara Museum of Art, "Attitudes: Photography in the 1970's," 1979.

Peter Lodato

Born in Los Angeles, 1946
Studied at San Fernando Valley State College, Northridge, California (B.F.A., 1969)
Lives in Los Angeles

SELECTED SOLO EXHIBITIONS: Brand Library Art Center, Glendale, California, 1971; Michael Walls Gallery, Los Angeles, 1973; University of California, Irvine, 1975; Claire Copley Gallery, Los Angeles, 1976; P.S. 1, Institute for Art and Urban Resources, Long Island City, New York, 1978; Rosamund Felsen Gallery, Los Angeles, 1978, 1980.

SELECTED GROUP EXHIBITIONS: Los Angeles County Museum of Art, "Twenty-four Los Angeles Artists," 1971; University of California, Santa Barbara, "Los Angeles Painting," 1972; San Francisco Museum of Modern Art, "Eight Los Angeles Artists," 1973; Los Angeles Institute of Contemporary Art, "100+—Current Directions in Southern California Art," 1977; Minneapolis College of Art and Design, "Bruce Nauman and Peter Lodato," 1978; Los Angeles Institute of Contemporary Art, "John McLaughlin, James Hayward and Peter Lodato," 1979.

Kim MacConnel

Born in Oklahoma City, 1946
Studied at the University of California, San Diego (B.A., 1969; M.F.A., 1972)
Lives in Encinitas, California

SELECTED SOLO EXHIBITIONS: Holly Solomon Gallery, New York 1975–76 (traveled nationally); Galerie Ehrensperger, Zurich, 1976; Holly Solomon Gallery,

1977, 1978; University Art Museum, University of California, Berkeley, 1978; Galerie Bischofsberger, Zurich, 1978; Mayor Gallery, London, 1978; Holly Solomon Gallery, 1979; Dart Gallery, Chicago, 1979, 1980; Holly Solomon Gallery, 1980.

SELECTED GROUP EXHIBITIONS: University of California, San Diego, "Decorations," 1971; Whitney Museum of American Art, New York, 1975 Biennial Exhibition; P.S. 1, Institute for Art and Urban Resources, Long Island City, New York, "Pattern Painting," 1977; Institute of Contemporary Art of The University of Pennsylvania, Philadelphia, "Improbable Furniture," 1977 (traveled nationally); La Jolla Museum of Contemporary Art, California, "Southern California Styles of the 60's and 70's," 1978; Contemporary Arts Center, Cincinnati, "Arabesque," 1978; Whitney Museum of American Art, 1979 Biennial Exhibition; Institute of Contemporary Art of The University of Pennsylvania, "The Decorative Impulse," 1979 (traveled nationally); Hirshhorn Museum and Sculpture Garden, Smithsonian Institution, Washington, D.C., "Directions," 1979; Galerie Krinzinger, Innsbruck, Austria, "Pattern Painting/Decoration Art," 1979; XIII Winter Olympic Games, Lake Placid, New York, "American Painting," 1980; 39th Venice Biennale, 1980.

Robert Mapplethorpe

Born in New York, 1946
Studied at Pratt Institute, Brooklyn, New York (1963–70)
Lives in New York

SELECTED SOLO EXHIBITIONS: Light Gallery, New York, 1976; Holly Solomon Gallery, New York, 1977; The Kitchen Center for Video, Music and Dance, New York, 1977; Corcoran Gallery of Art, Washington, D.C., 1978; Simon Lowinsky Gallery, San Francisco, 1978; Langdon Street Gallery, San Francisco, 1978; La Remise du Parc Gallery, Paris, 1978; Robert Miller Gallery, New York, 1979; Texas Gallery, Houston, 1979; In A Plain Brown Wrapper, Chicago, 1980; Jurka Galerie, Amsterdam, 1980.

SELECTED GROUP EXHIBITIONS: Corcoran Gallery of Art, Washington, D.C., "The Collection of Sam Wagstaff," 1977–78 (traveled nationally); Kassel, West Germany, Documenta 6, 1977; The Museum of Modern Art, New York, "Mirrors and Windows: American Photography Since 1960," 1978; Whitney Museum of American Art, New York, Downtown Branch, "Artists by Artists," 1979; Santa Barbara Museum of Art, California, "Attitudes: Photography in the 1970's," 1979; Jehu Gallery, San Francisco, "Secret Paintings (Erotic Paintings and Photographs)," 1980; Carson-Sapiro Gallery, Denver, "New Visions," 1980.

Joel Meyerowitz

Born in New York, 1938
Studied at Ohio State University, Columbus (B.F.A., 1959)
Lives in New York

SELECTED SOLO EXHIBITIONS: International Museum of Photography at George Eastman House, Rochester, New York, 1966; The Museum of Modern Art, New York, 1968; Museum of Fine Arts, Boston, 1978 (traveled nationally); Akron Art Institute, Akron, Ohio, 1979; The St. Louis Art Museum, 1980.

SELECTED GROUP EXHIBITIONS: The Museum of Modern Art, New York, "The Photographer's Eye," 1963; The Museum of Modern Art, New York, "Portraits," 1970; Osaka, Japan, Expo 70, "10 Americans," 1970; Carpenter Center, Harvard University, Cambridge, Massachusetts, "Wedding Group," 1976; The Art Museum, Princeton University, Princeton, New Jersey, "Twentieth-Century Photographs," 1976; Museum of Fine Arts, Boston, "Inner Light," 1977; The Museum of Modern Art, New York, "Mirrors and Windows: American Photography Since 1960," 1978.

Duane Michals

Born in McKeesport, Pennsylvania, 1932
Studied at the University of Denver (B.A., 1953)
Lives in New York

SELECTED SOLO EXHIBITIONS: Underground Gallery, New York, 1963, 1965, 1968; The Art Institute of Chicago, 1968; Light Gallery, New York, 1974; G. Ray

Michals *(cont.)*

Hawkins Gallery, Los Angeles, 1977; Sidney Janis Gallery, New York, 1978; Nouvelles Images, The Hague, 1979; Museo de Arte Moderno, Bogota, Colombia, 1980; Sidney Janis Gallery, 1980.

SELECTED GROUP EXHIBITIONS: Image Gallery, New York, 1959; Hayden Gallery, Massachusetts Institute of Technology, Cambridge, "Being Without Clothes," 1970; Whitney Museum of American Art, New York, "Photography in America," 1974; Whitney Museum of American Art, 1977 Biennial Exhibition; Contemporary Arts Museum, Houston, "American Narrative/Story Art," 1977; Whitney Museum of American Art, "Art About Art," 1978; The New Gallery, Cleveland, "Photographic Surrealism," 1979 (traveled nationally).

Richard Misrach

Born in Los Angeles, 1949
Studied at the University of California, Berkeley (B.A., 1971)
Lives in Berkeley

SELECTED SOLO EXHIBITIONS: International Center of Photography, New York, 1975; Madison Art Center, Madison, Wisconsin, 1976; Atlantic Richfield Company (ARCO) Center for Visual Arts, Los Angeles, 1977; The Oakland Museum, Oakland, California, 1977; Grapestake Gallery, San Francisco, 1979; Musée National d'Art Moderne, Centre National d'Art et de Culture Georges Pompidou, Paris, 1979; Silver Image Gallery, Seattle, Washington, 1980; G. Ray Hawkins Gallery, Los Angeles, 1980.

SELECTED GROUP EXHIBITIONS: Fogg Art Museum, Harvard University, Cambridge, Massachusetts, "Contemporary Photography," 1976; The Oakland Museum, Oakland, California, "Night Landscape," 1977; The Museum of Modern Art, New York, "Mirrors and Windows: American Photography Since 1960," 1978; Santa Barbara Museum of Art, California, "Attitudes: Photography in the 1970's," 1979; Corcoran Gallery of Art, Washington, D.C., "American Images," 1979 (traveled nationally); Milwaukee Art Center, "Color: A Spectrum of Recent Photography/Part II: The Romantic Vision and Beyond," 1979; San Francisco Museum of Modern Art, "Beyond Color," 1979; Sewall Art Gallery, Rice University, Houston, "Recent Color Photography," 1980.

Mary Miss

Born in New York, 1941
Studied at the University of California, Santa Barbara (B.A., 1966); Rinehart School of Sculpture, Maryland Art Institute, Baltimore (M.F.A., 1968)
Lives in New York

SELECTED SOLO EXHIBITIONS AND INSTALLATIONS: 55 Mercer Gallery, New York, 1971; Allen Memorial Art Museum, Oberlin College, Oberlin, Ohio, *Untitled*, 1973 (site installation); Battery Park City Landfill, New York, *Untitled*, 1973 (site installation); Rosa Esman Gallery, New York, 1975; The Museum of Modern Art, New York, 1976; Nassau County Museum of Fine Arts, Roslyn, New York, *Perimeters/Pavilions/Decoys* (site installation), 1978; Dayton, Ohio, *Staged Gates*, 1979 (site installation); Max Protetch Gallery, New York, 1980; Fogg Art Museum, Harvard University, Cambridge, Massachusetts, 1980.

SELECTED GROUP EXHIBITIONS AND INSTALLATIONS: Whitney Museum of American Art, New York, "Annual Exhibition: Contemporary American Sculpture," 1970; Whitney Museum of American Art, 1973 Biennial Exhibition; Allen Memorial Art Museum, Oberlin College, Oberlin, Ohio, "Four Young Americans," 1973; P.S. 1, Institute for Art and Urban Resources, Long Island City, New York, "Rooms," 1976; The Solomon R. Guggenheim Museum, New York, "Nine Artists: The Theodoran Awards," 1977; Whitney Museum of American Art, Downtown Branch, "Architectural Analogues," 1978; XIII Winter Olympic Games, Lake Placid, New York, "Environmental Art," *Veiled Landscape*, 1979 (site installation); 39th Venice Biennale, 1980; Indianapolis Museum of Art, "Painting and Sculpture Today, 1980," 1980; Los Angeles Institute of Contemporary Art, "Architectural Sculpture," 1980.

Owen Morrel

Born in New York, 1950
Studied at Colgate University, Hamilton, New York (1968–71)
Lives in New York

SELECTED SOLO EXHIBITIONS AND INSTALLATIONS: Gallery of the School of Visual Arts, New York, 1974; Poughkeepsie, New York, *Telescopic Reference Points*, 1975 (site installation); Brooklyn, New York, *Desk Axis*, 1975–76 (site installation); New York, *Catapult*, 1977 (site installation); American Thread Building, New York, *Asylum*, 1978–79 (site installation); Galerie Schmela, Düsseldorf, West Germany, 1979; Galerie Yvon Lambert, Paris, 1979; Artpark, Lewiston, New York, *Omega*, 1980 (site installation); Galerie Schmela, 1980; Galerie Yvon Lambert, 1980.

Robert Moskowitz

Born in New York, 1935
Self-taught
Lives in New York

SELECTED SOLO EXHIBITIONS: Leo Castelli Gallery, New York, 1962; French & Company, New York, 1970; Hayden Gallery, Massachusetts Institute of Technology, Cambridge, 1971; Nancy Hoffman Gallery, New York, 1973, 1974; The Clocktower, Institute for Art and Urban Resources, New York, 1977; Daniel Weinberg Gallery, San Francisco, 1979; Margo Leavin Gallery, Los Angeles, 1979; La Jolla Museum of Contemporary Art, California, 1979; Daniel Weinberg Gallery, 1980; Margo Leavin Gallery, 1980.

SELECTED GROUP EXHIBITIONS: The Museum of Modern Art, New York, "Art of Assemblage," 1961; Whitney Museum of American Art, New York, "Annual Exhibition: Contemporary American Painting," 1969; Whitney Museum of American Art, 1973 Biennial Exhibition; Paula Cooper Gallery, New York, 1976, 1977; Willard Gallery, New York, 1978; Whitney Museum of American Art, "New Image Painting," 1978; Albright-Knox Art Gallery, Buffalo, New York, "American Painting of the 1970's," 1978; Whitney Museum of American Art, 1979 Biennial Exhibition; Whitney Museum of American Art, "Decade in Review," 1979; 39th Venice Biennale, 1980; Padiglione d'Arte Contemporanea, Milan, "Pictures in New York Today," 1980; Indianapolis Museum of Art, "Painting and Sculpture Today," 1980.

Grant Mudford

Born in Sydney, Australia, 1944
Studied at University of New South Wales, Sydney, Australia (1963–64)
Lives in Los Angeles

SELECTED SOLO EXHIBITIONS: Bonython Gallery, Sydney, Australia, 1972; Light Gallery, New York, 1976, 1977; Hirshhorn Museum and Sculpture Garden, Smithsonian Institution, Washington, D.C., 1979; Diane Brown Gallery, Washington, D.C., 1979; Rosamund Felsen Gallery, Los Angeles, 1979; Light Gallery, 1979.

SELECTED GROUP EXHIBITIONS: Australian Center For Photography, Sydney, "Aspects of Australian Photography," 1974–75 (traveled nationally); Victoria and Albert Museum, London, "The Land—20th Century Landscape Photographs," 1975–76 (traveled internationally); Light Gallery, New York, "New York, New York," 1978; Whitney Museum of American Art, New York, Downtown Branch, "Industrial Sights," 1979; Santa Barbara Museum of Art, California, "Attitudes: Photography in the 1970's," 1979.

Elizabeth Murray

Born in Chicago, 1940
Studied at the School of The Art Institute of Chicago (B.F.A., 1962); Mills College, Oakland, California (M.F.A., 1964)
Lives in New York

SELECTED SOLO EXHIBITIONS: Paula Cooper Gallery, New York, 1975; The Jared Sable Gallery, Toronto, 1975; Paula Cooper Gallery, 1976; Phyllis Kind Gallery, Chicago, 1978; Paula Cooper Gallery, 1978; Galerie Mukai, Tokyo, 1980.

Murray *(cont.)*

SELECTED GROUP EXHIBITIONS: Whitney Museum of American Art, New York, "Annual Exhibition: Contemporary American Painting," 1972; Whitney Museum of American Art, 1973 Biennial Exhibition; California State University, Los Angeles, "New Work/New York," 1976; The Solomon R. Guggenheim Museum, New York, "Nine Artists; The Theodoran Awards," 1977; New York State Museum, Albany, "New York: The State of Art," 1977; The New Museum, New York, "Early Work by Five Contemporary Artists," 1977; Hayward Gallery, London, "New Painting, New York," 1979; Whitney Museum of American Art, "The Decade in Review," 1979; Whitney Museum of American Art, 1979 Biennial Exhibition.

Andrew Noren

Born in Santa Fe, New Mexico, 1943
Lives in New York

SELECTED SOLO EXHIBITIONS: The Art Institute of Chicago Film Center, 1974; Collective for Living Cinema, New York, 1974; Anthology Film Archives, New York, 1974; Whitney Museum of American Art, New York, New American Filmmakers Series, 1974; The Museum of Modern Art, New York, 1975; Whitney Museum of American Art, New American Filmmakers Series, 1976; Walker Art Center, Minneapolis, 1977; The Art Institute of Chicago Film Center, 1977; Anthology Film Archives, 1977; The Museum of Modern Art, New York, 1979.

SELECTED GROUP EXHIBITIONS: National Film Theater of London, "International Avant-Garde Film Festival," 1973; State University of New York, Buffalo, "Conference on Autobiographical Cinema," 1973; Moderna Museet, Stockholm, "The Pleasure Dome: American Experimental Film," 1980.

Arthur Ollman

Born in Milwaukee, Wisconsin, 1947
Studied at the University of Wisconsin, Madison (B.A., 1969); Lone Mountain College, San Francisco (M.F.A., 1977)
Lives in Oakland, California

SELECTED SOLO EXHIBITIONS: Atlantic Richfield Company (ARCO) Center for Visual Art, Los Angeles, 1978; Camera Obscura Gallery, Stockholm, 1979; Grapestake Gallery, San Francisco, 1979; Musée National d'Art Moderne, Centre National d'Art et de Culture Georges Pompidou, Paris, 1979.

SELECTED GROUP EXHIBITIONS: Camerawork Gallery, San Francisco, "Contemporary California Photography," 1978; Santa Barbara Museum of Art, California, "Attitudes: Photography in the 1970's," 1979; Milwaukee Art Center, "Color: A Spectrum of Recent Photography/Part II: Romantic Vision and Beyond," 1979; The Museum of Modern Art, New York, "Mirrors and Windows: American Photography Since 1960," 1979; University of Hawaii, Honolulu, "Spectrum: New Directions in Color Photography," 1979 (traveled nationally).

Dennis Oppenheim

Born in Mason City (now Electric City), Washington, 1938
Studied at the California College of Arts and Crafts, Oakland (B.F.A., 1965); Stanford University, Palo Alto, California (M.F.A., 1965)
Lives in New York

SELECTED SOLO EXHIBITIONS: John Gibson Gallery, New York, 1968, 1969, 1970; Museum of Conceptual Art, San Francisco, 1973; Stedelijk Museum, Amsterdam, 1974; Hans Meyer Gallery, Düsseldorf, West Germany, 1977; University of Rhode Island Gallery, Kingston, 1977; Musée d'Art Contemporain, Montreal, 1978; Kunsthalle Basel, Switzerland, 1979; Kunstverein Stuttgart, West Germany, 1979; Cranbrook Academy of Art/Museum, Bloomfield Hills, Michigan, 1980; Ace Gallery, Los Angeles, 1980; Portland Center for the Visual Arts, Oregon, 1980.

SELECTED GROUP EXHIBITIONS: Andrew Dickson White Museum of Art, Cornell University, Ithaca, New York, "Earth Art," 1969; The Museum of Modern Art, New York, "Information," 1970; Whitney Museum of American Art, New York, "Annual Exhibition: Contemporary American Sculpture," 1970; Whitney Museum of

American Art, "American Drawings," 1973; Hayden Gallery, Massachusetts Institute of Technology, Cambridge, "Interventions in Landscape," 1974; The Clocktower, Institute for Art and Urban Resources, New York, "Words and Works," 1974; Museum of Contemporary Art, Chicago, "Body Art," 1975; Sterling and Francine Clark Art Institute, Williamstown, Massachusetts, "The Dada Surrealist Heritage," 1977; The New Museum, New York, "Early Works by Five Contemporary Artists," 1977; Whitney Museum of American Art, 1977 Biennial Exhibition; Whitney Museum of American Art, Downtown Branch, "Words," 1977; Museum of Contemporary Art, Chicago, "A View of a Decade," 1977; Customs House, New York, "Custom and Culture," 1979; Musée National d'Art Moderne, Centre National d'Art et de Culture Georges Pompidou, Paris, "Video Art," 1979; Museum of Contemporary Art, Chicago, "Concept, Narrative, Document," 1979; Sonnabend Gallery, New York, "Morris, Acconci, Oppenheim," 1980; Los Angeles Institute of Contemporary Art, "Architectural Sculpture," 1980; 39th Venice Biennale, 1980.

Nam June Paik

Born in Seoul, Korea, 1932
Studied at the University of Tokyo (B.A., 1956); University of Munich, Freiburg Conservatory, and the University of Cologne (1956–58)
Lives in New York

Selected Solo Exhibitions: Galerie 22, Düsseldorf, West Germany, 1959; Galerie Parnass, Wuppertal, West Germany, 1963; Sogetsu Hall, Tokyo, 1964; Galeria Bonino, New York, 1965, 1968, 1976; Everson Museum of Art, Syracuse, New York, 1976; Rene Block Gallery, New York, 1976; Carnegie Hall, New York, 1977; WDR-TV, Cologne, West Germany, 1977 (broadcast); The Museum of Modern Art, New York, 1977; Galerie Watari, Tokyo, 1978; Centre National d'Art et de Culture Georges Pompidou, Paris, 1978; Musée d'Art Moderne de la Ville de Paris, 1978; Whitney Museum of American Art, New York, New American Filmmakers Series, 1980; Galerie Watari, 1980.

Selected Group Exhibitions: Museum Wiesbaden, West Germany, "Fluxus Festival," 1962; The Museum of Modern Art, New York, "Machine Show," 1968; Howard Wise Gallery, New York, "TV as a Creative Medium," 1969; Kunstverein, Cologne, West Germany, "Fluxus Happening," 1970; XIII Bienal de São Paolo, 1975; Kassel, West Germany, Documenta 6, 1977; Kunstverein, Cologne, "Comprehensive Video Show," 1977; The Solomon R. Guggenheim Museum, New York, "Intermedia Festival," 1980.

Ed Paschke

Born in Chicago, 1939
Studied at the School of The Art Institute of Chicago (B.F.A., 1961; M.A., 1970)
Lives in Chicago

Selected Solo Exhibitions: Deson-Zaks Gallery, Chicago, 1970; Hundred Acres Gallery, New York, 1971; Deson-Zaks Gallery, 1972, 1973; Galerie Darthea Speyer, Paris, 1974; Hundred Acres Gallery, 1974; Contemporary Arts Center, Cincinnati, 1974; Deson-Zaks Gallery, 1975; Pyramid Gallery, Washington, D.C., 1975; Galerie Darthea Speyer, 1976; Phyllis Kind Gallery, Chicago, 1977; Galerie Darthea Speyer, 1978; Phyllis Kind Gallery, New York, 1978, 1979; Phyllis Kind Gallery, Chicago, 1979; Phyllis Kind Gallery, New York, 1980.

Selected Group Exhibitions: Whitney Museum of American Art, New York, "Human Concern/Personal Torment: The Grotesque in American Art," 1969; Institute of Contemporary Art of The University of Pennsylvania, Philadelphia, "Spirit of the Comics," 1969; Museum of Contemporary Art, Chicago, "Chicago Imagist Art," 1972; The National Gallery of Canada, Ottawa, organizer, "What They're Up To In Chicago," 1972–73 (traveled nationally); XII Bienal de São Paolo, "Made in Chicago," 1973 (traveled internationally); E.B. Crocker Art Gallery, Sacramento, California, "The Chicago Connection," 1977 (traveled nationally); Museum of Contemporary Art, Chicago, "View of a Decade," 1977; Aspen Center for Visual Arts, Colorado, "American Portraits of the Sixties and Seventies," 1979; Mayor Gallery, London, "Six Artists from Chicago," 1980; Sunderland Museum & Art Gallery, England, "Who Chicago? An Exhibition of Contemporary Imagists," 1980.

Judy Pfaff

Born in London, 1946
Studied at Wayne State University, Detroit (1965–66); Southern Illinois University, Edwardsville (1968–69); Washington University, St. Louis (B.F.A., 1971); Yale University Summer School of Music and Art, Norfolk, Connecticut (1970); Yale University, New Haven, Connecticut (M.F.A., 1973)
Lives in New York

Selected Solo Exhibitions: Webb and Parsons Gallery, New Canaan, Connecticut, 1974; Artists Space, New York, 1975; Theatre Gallery, University of Southern Florida, Tampa, 1977; Los Angeles Contemporary Exhibitions (LACE), 1978; Holly Solomon Gallery, New York, 1980.

Selected Group Exhibitions: Whitney Museum of American Art, New York, 1975 Biennial Exhibition; Hallwalls Gallery, Buffalo, New York, "Approaching Painting: Part Three," 1976; Art Museum, University of California, Santa Barbara, "Sculptural Perspectives," 1979; Neuberger Museum, State University of New York, College at Purchase, "Ten Artists/Artists Space," 1979; Contemporary Arts Museum, Houston, "Extensions: Jennifer Bartlett, Lynda Benglis, Robert Longo, Judy Pfaff," 1980; Contemporary Arts Center, Cincinnati, "Walls," 1980.

Katherine Porter

Born in Cedar Rapids, Iowa, 1941
Studied at Colorado College, Colorado Springs (B.A., 1963); Boston University (1962)
Lives in Lincolnville, Maine

Selected Solo Exhibitions: University of Rhode Island, Kingston, 1971; Henri Gallery, Washington, D.C., 1972; Worcester Art Museum, Massachusetts, 1973; Hayden Gallery, Massachusetts Institute of Technology, Cambridge, 1974; David McKee Gallery, New York, 1975; Harkus Krakow Gallery, Boston, 1976; David McKee Gallery, 1978, 1979; San Francisco Museum of Modern Art, 1980 (traveled nationally).

Selected Group Exhibitions: Whitney Museum of American Art, New York, "Annual Exhibition: Contemporary American Painting," 1969; Hayden Gallery, Massachusetts Institute of Technology, Cambridge, "Six Artists," 1970; Whitney Museum of American Art, 1973 Biennial Exhibition; The Solomon R. Guggenheim Museum, New York, "Nine Artists: The Theodoran Awards," 1977; Otis Art Institute, Los Angeles, "New York—A Selection From the Last 10 Years," 1979; XIII Winter Olympic Games, Lake Placid, New York, "American Painting," 1980; Milwaukee Art Center, "Art in Our Time: HHK Foundation for Contemporary Art, Inc.," 1980 (traveled nationally).

Kenneth Price

Born in Los Angeles, 1935
Studied at Chouinard Art Institute, Los Angeles (1953–54); University of Southern California, Los Angeles (B.F.A., 1956); Otis Art Institute, Los Angeles (1957–58); State University of New York, Alfred (M.F.A., 1959)
Lives in Taos, New Mexico

Selected Solo Exhibitions: Ferus Gallery, Los Angeles, 1960, 1961, 1964; Kasmin Gallery, London, 1968; Whitney Museum of American Art, New York, 1969; Nicholas Wilder Gallery, Los Angeles, 1973; Felicity Samuel Gallery, London, 1974; Willard Gallery, New York, 1974; James Corcoran Gallery, Los Angeles, 1976; Los Angeles County Museum of Art, 1978; Willard Gallery, 1979; Gallery of the School of Visual Arts, New York, 1980.

Selected Group Exhibitions: Whitney Museum of American Art, New York, "Fifty California Artists," 1962; Pasadena Art Museum, California, "New American Sculpture," 1964; Los Angeles County Museum of Art, "Robert Irwin/Kenneth Price," 1966; Los Angeles County Museum of Art, "American Sculpture of the Sixties," 1967; University of California, Irvine, "Abstract Expressionist Ceramics," 1967; The National Museum of Modern Art, Kyoto, Japan, "Contemporary Ceramic Art: Canada, U.S.A., Mexico, and Japan," 1971; The Museum of Modern Art, New York, "Gemini: Technics and Creativity," 1971; Whitney Museum of

American Art, Downtown Branch, "Clay," 1974; Whitney Museum of American Art, "200 Years of American Sculpture," 1976; San Francisco Museum of Modern Art, "Painting and Sculpture in California: The Modern Era," 1976 (traveled nationally); Everson Museum of Art, Syracuse, New York, "A Century of Ceramics in the United States, 1878–1978," 1979 (traveled nationally); Whitney Museum of American Art, 1979 Biennial Exhibition.

Martin Puryeur

Born in Washington, D.C., 1941
Studied at the Catholic University of America, Washington, D.C. (B.A., 1963); Swedish Royal Academy of Art, Stockholm (1966–68); Yale University, New Haven, Connecticut (M.F.A., 1971)
Lives in Chicago

SELECTED SOLO EXHIBITIONS: Grona Palletten Gallery, Stockholm, 1968; Fisk University, Nashville, Tennessee, 1972; Henri Gallery, Washington, D.C., 1972, 1973; Corcoran Gallery of Art, Washington, D.C., 1977; Protetch-McIntosh Gallery, Washington, D.C., 1978; Museum of Contemporary Art, Chicago, 1980; Young-Hoffman Gallery, Chicago, 1980.

SELECTED GROUP EXHIBITIONS: Artpark, Lewiston, New York, 1977; The Solomon R. Guggenheim Museum, New York, "Young American Artists," 1978; Whitney Museum of American Art, New York, 1979 Biennial Exhibition; Wave Hill, Bronx, New York, "Wave Hill: The Artist's View," 1979; P.S. 1, Institute for Art and Urban Resources, Long Island City, New York, "Afro-American Abstraction," 1980.

Yvonne Rainer

Born in San Francisco, 1934
Studied at San Francisco City College (1952–53)
Lives in New York

SELECTED SOLO EXHIBITIONS: Pacific Film Archive, University Art Museum, Berkeley, California, 1975; Walker Art Center, Minneapolis, 1975; Whitney Museum of American Art, New York, New American Filmmakers Series, 1976; The Museum of Modern Art, New York, 1976, 1977; The Other Cinema, London, 1977; Media Study, Buffalo, New York, 1979; Walker Art Center, 1979; Bleecker Street Cinema, New York, 1980; Anthology Film Archives, New York, 1980; The Art Institute of Chicago Film Center, 1980; National Gallery of Canada, Ottawa, 1980.

SELECTED GROUP EXHIBITIONS: Whitney Museum of American Art, New York, New American Filmmakers Series, "Women's Film Festival," 1973; National Film Theater, London, "Festival of Avant-Garde Cinema," 1973; Montreux, Switzerland, "New Forms in Film," 1974; Edinburgh International Film Festival, 1975; Berlin Film Festival, West Berlin, 1975; Edinburgh International Film Festival, 1976; Berlin Film Festival, 1977, 1980; Edinburgh International Film Festival, 1980; Festival International du Nouveau Cinéma, Montreal, 1980.

Leland Rice

Born in Los Angeles, 1940
Studied at Arizona State University, Tempe (B.S., 1964); Chouinard Art Institute, Los Angeles (1965); California State University, San Francisco (M.A., 1969)
Lives in Los Angeles

SELECTED SOLO EXHIBITIONS: Friends of Photography, Carmel, California, 1972; Witkin Gallery, New York, 1973; School of The Art Institute of Chicago, 1974; Jack Glenn Gallery, Newport Beach, California, 1976; Hirshhorn Museum and Sculpture Garden, Smithsonian Institution, Washington, D.C., 1977 (traveled nationally); Diane Brown Gallery, Washington, D.C., 1977; Rosamund Felsen Gallery, Los Angeles, 1979; Grapestake Gallery, San Francisco, 1980.

SELECTED GROUP EXHIBITIONS: Memorial Union Art Gallery, University of California, Davis, "California Photographers," 1970 (traveled nationally); Whitney Museum of American Art, New York, "Photography in America," 1974; The Museum of Modern Art, New York, "Mirrors and Windows: American Photography

Rice *(cont.)*

Since 1960," 1978; De Cordova and Dana Museum and Park, Lincoln, Massachusetts, "Aspects of the 70's: Photography—Recent Directions," 1980; Milwaukee Art Center, "Art in Our Time: The Collection of the HHK Foundation of Contemporary Art," 1980 (traveled nationally).

Bruce Robbins

Born in Philadelphia, 1948
Studied at Hebrew University, Jerusalem (1968–69); Temple University, Philadelphia (B.A., 1970); Cooper Union, New York (B.F.A., 1973)
Lives in New York

Selected Solo Exhibitions: Truman Gallery, New York, 1977, 1978, 1979; Blum/Helman Gallery, New York, 1979.

Selected Group Exhibitions: Weatherspoon Gallery, Greensboro, North Carolina, "Invitational," 1976; Parsons-Truman Gallery, New York, "This Doesn't Look Like A Work of Art," 1976; Organization of Independent Artists, New York, "Constructions," 1978; Freedman Gallery, Albright College, Reading, Pennsylvania, "Small is Beautiful," 1979; Audrey Strohl Gallery, Memphis, Tennessee, 1979; 39th Venice Biennale, 1980; Stedelijk Museum, Amsterdam, "Recent Acquisitions," 1980.

James Rosenquist

Born in Grand Forks, North Dakota, 1933
Studied at the University of Minnesota, Minneapolis (1952–54); The Art Students League of New York (1955)
Lives in New York and Aripeka, Florida

Selected Solo Exhibitions: Green Gallery, New York, 1962, 1963, 1964; Dwan Gallery, Los Angeles, 1964; Leo Castelli Gallery, New York, 1965, 1966; Moderna Museet, Stockholm, 1966; Stedelijk Museum, Amsterdam, 1966; Kunsthalle Bern, Switzerland, 1966; Louisiana Museum, Humlebaek, Denmark, 1966; Leo Castelli Gallery, 1969, 1970; Wallraf-Richartz Museum, Cologne, West Germany, 1972; Whitney Museum of American Art, New York, 1972; Museum of Contemporary Art, Chicago, 1972; Leo Castelli Gallery, 1973; Stedelijk Museum, 1973; Leo Castelli Gallery, 1977; Castelli Feigen Corcoran, New York, 1980.

Selected Group Exhibitions: Sidney Janis Gallery, New York, "New Realists," 1962; The Museum of Modern Art, New York, "Sixteen Americans," 1963; Institute of Contemporary Arts, London, "The Popular Image," 1963; The Art Institute of Chicago, "Sixty-eighth American Exhibition," 1966; Kassel, West Germany, Documenta 4, 1968; Hayward Gallery, London, "Pop Art," 1969; The Metropolitan Museum of Art, New York, "New York Painting and Sculpture: 1940–1970," 1969–70; Sterling and Francine Clark Art Institute, Williamstown, Massachusetts, "The Dada/Surrealist Heritage," 1977; Albright-Knox Art Gallery, Buffalo, New York, "American Painting of the 1970s," 1978 (traveled nationally); The Denver Art Museum, "Poets and Painters," 1979; Chrysler Museum at Norfolk, Virginia, "American Figure Painting 1950–1980," 1980.

Julian Schnabel

Born in New York, 1951
Studied at the University of Houston (B.F.A., 1972); Whitney Museum of American Art Independent Study Program, New York (1973–74)
Lives in New York

Selected Solo Exhibitions: Contemporary Arts Museum, Houston, 1976; Mary Boone Gallery, New York, 1979; Daniel Weinberg Gallery, San Francisco, 1979; Mary Boone Gallery, 1979; Young-Hoffman Gallery, Chicago, 1980.

Selected Group Exhibitions: Renaissance Society at the University of Chicago, "Visionary Images," 1979; Hallwalls Gallery, Buffalo, New York, "Four Artists," 1979; Grand Palais, Paris, "L'Amérique aux Indépendants," 1980; 39th Venice Biennale, 1980.

Victor Schrager

Born in Bethesda, Maryland, 1950
Studied at Harvard University, Cambridge, Massachusetts (B.A., 1972); Florida State University, Tallahassee (M.F.A., 1975)
Lives in New York

SELECTED SOLO EXHIBITIONS: Robert Freidus Gallery, New York, 1978; Sander Gallery, Washington, D.C., 1979; Robert Freidus Gallery, 1979; Los Angeles Institute of Contemporary Art, 1979; Northlight Gallery, Tempe, Arizona, 1979.

SELECTED GROUP EXHIBITIONS: Gallery 413, Atlanta College of Art, "Optional Narrative," 1976; Jacksonville Art Museum, Florida, "Florida Photographers," 1976; Tyler School of Art, Temple University, Philadelphia, "Southern Fried," 1977; San Francisco Museum of Modern Art, "Fabricated to be Photographed," 1979; Light Gallery, New York, "20 x 24 Polaroid," 1979 (traveled nationally); De Cordova and Dana Museum and Park, Lincoln, Massachusetts, "Aspects of the 70's: Photography—Recent Directions," 1980.

Buky Schwartz

Born in Jerusalem, 1932
Studied at the Avni School of Fine Arts, Tel Aviv (1957–59); St. Martin's School of Art, London (1959–62)
Lives in New York

SELECTED SOLO EXHIBITIONS: 33rd Venice Biennale, 1966; Tel Aviv Museum, 1968; Israel Museum, Jerusalem, 1970; International Cultural Centre, Antwerp, 1978; O.K. Harris Gallery, New York, 1978; Akron Art Institute, Akron, Ohio, 1978; XIII Winter Olympic Games, Lake Placid, New York, 1980.

SELECTED GROUP EXHIBITIONS: Israel Museum, Jerusalem, "Beyond Drawing," 1974; Indianapolis Museum of Art, "Painting and Sculpture Today," 1976; Whitney Museum of American Art, New York, New American Filmmakers Series, "Re-Visions: Projects and Proposals in Film and Video," 1979; International Cultural Centre, Antwerp, "Beyond Surface," 1980.

Richard Serra

Born in San Francisco, 1939
Studied at the University of California, Berkeley and Santa Barbara (B.A., 1961); Yale University, New Haven, Connecticut (M.F.A., 1964)
Lives in New York

SELECTED SOLO EXHIBITIONS: Galerie Ricke, Cologne, West Germany, 1968; Castelli Warehouse, New York, 1969–70; Pasadena Art Museum, California, 1970; Ace Gallery, Los Angeles, 1970, 1972; Galleria Toselli, Milan, 1973; Leo Castelli Gallery, New York, 1974; Portland Center for the Visual Arts, Oregon, 1975; Galerie Daniel Templon, Paris, 1977; Stedelijk Museum, Amsterdam, 1977; Staatliche Kunsthalle Baden-Baden, West Germany, 1978; Blum/Helman Gallery, New York, 1978; The Hudson River Museum, Yonkers, New York, 1980.

SELECTED GROUP EXHIBITIONS: Noah Goldowsky Gallery, New York, "Arp to Artschwager," 1967; Noah Goldowsky Gallery, "Three Sculptors," 1968; Castelli Warehouse, New York, "Nine at Castelli," 1968; The Museum of Modern Art, New York, "New Media: New Methods," 1969 (traveled nationally); Stedelijk Museum, Amsterdam, "Square Pegs in Round Holes," 1969 (traveled internationally); Kunsthalle Bern, Switzerland, "When Attitudes Become Form," 1969 (traveled internationally); Whitney Museum of American Art, New York "Anti-Illusion: Procedures/Materials," 1969; The Solomon R. Guggenheim Museum, New York, "Nine Artists: The Theodoran Awards," 1969; Tokyo Metropolitan Art Museum, "Between Man and Matter, 19th Tokyo Biennale '70," 1970; The Museum of Modern Art, New York, "Information," 1970; The Solomon R. Guggenheim Museum, "Sixth International Guggenheim Exhibition," 1971; Walker Art Center, Minneapolis, "Works for New Spaces," 1971; Los Angeles County Museum of Art, "Art and Technology," 1971; The Art Museum, Princeton University, Princeton, New Jersey, "Line as Language: Six Artists Draw," 1974; Hayward Gallery, London, "The Condition of Sculpture—A Selection of Sculpture by Younger British and Foreign Artists," 1975; Whitney Museum of American Art, "200 Years of American

Serra *(cont.)*

Sculpture," 1976; Stedelijk Museum, "Made by Sculptors," 1978; Museum Haus Lange, Krefeld, West Germany, "The Broadening Concept of Reality: The Art of the 60s and 70s," 1979; Hayden Gallery, Massachusetts Institute of Technology, Cambridge, "Bochner/Serra," 1980.

Joel Shapiro

Born in New York, 1941
Studied at New York University (B.A., 1964; M.A., 1969)
Lives in New York

SELECTED SOLO EXHIBITIONS: Paula Cooper Gallery, New York, 1970, 1972; The Clocktower, Institute of Art and Urban Resources, New York, 1973; Paula Cooper Gallery, 1974, 1975; Museum of Contemporary Art, Chicago, 1976; Albright-Knox Art Gallery, Buffalo, New York, 1977; Paula Cooper Gallery, 1977; Akron Art Institute, Akron, Ohio, 1979; Paula Cooper Gallery, 1979; Whitechapel Art Gallery, London, 1980 (traveled internationally); Brown University, Providence, Rhode Island, 1980; Paula Cooper Gallery, 1980.

SELECTED GROUP EXHIBITIONS: Whitney Museum of American Art, New York, "Anti-Illusion: Procedures/Materials," 1969; Whitney Museum of American Art, "Annual Exhibition: Contemporary American Sculpture," 1970; The Art Institute of Chicago, "Seventy-first American Exhibition," 1974; University Gallery, University of Massachusetts, Amherst, "Critical Perspectives in American Art," 1976 (traveled internationally); Whitney Museum of American Art, 1977 Biennial Exhibition; Kassel, West Germany, Documenta 6, 1977; Walker Art Center, Minneapolis, "Scale and Environment: 10 Sculptors," 1977; Stedelijk Museum, Amsterdam, "Made by Sculptors," 1978; Whitney Museum of American Art, 1979 Biennial Exhibition; Whitney Museum of American Art, "The Decade in Review: Selections from the 1970s," 1979; 39th Venice Biennale, 1980.

Sally Shapiro

Born in Los Angeles, 1947
Studied at San Diego State University (1965–67); University of California, Los Angeles (B.A., 1975)
Lives in New York

SELECTED SOLO EXHIBITIONS: Long Beach Museum of Art, California, 1978; The Museum of Modern Art, New York, 1978; Anthology Film Archives, New York, 1979.

SELECTED GROUP EXHIBITIONS: Long Beach Museum of Art, California, "Videoworks: Joel Herman, Sally Shapiro," 1978; Los Angeles Institute of Contemporary Art, "Public Domain/Private Shadows," 1978; The Kitchen Center for Video, Music and Dance, New York, "Video DJ Show," 1979; Ithaca Video Center, Ithaca, New York, "Ithaca Video Festival," 1979–80 (traveled nationally); The Museum of Modern Art, New York, "Video: New York, Seattle, Los Angeles," 1980 (traveled in Japan).

Paul Sharits

Born in Denver, 1943
Studied at the University of Denver (B.F.A., 1964); Indiana University (M.F.A., 1966)
Lives in Buffalo, New York

SELECTED SOLO EXHIBITIONS: The Museum of Modern Art, New York, 1968; Oesterreichisches Filmmuseum, Vienna, 1970; Bykert Gallery, New York, 1972; Anthology Film Archives, New York, 1972; Museum of Art, Carnegie Institute, Pittsburgh, 1973; Royal Film Archives, Brussels, 1973; Bykert Gallery, 1974; Whitney Museum of American Art, New York, New American Filmmakers Series, 1975; Albright-Knox Art Gallery, Buffalo, New York, 1976; Centre National d'Art et de Culture Georges Pompidou, Paris, 1977; Pacific Film Archive, University Art Museum, Berkeley, California, 1977; Anthology Film Archives, 1978; Art Gallery of Ontario, Toronto, 1978; "A" Gallery, Amsterdam, 1980.

Selected Group Exhibitions: Albright-Knox Art Gallery, Buffalo, New York, "Six Filmmakers," 1973; John F. Kennedy Center for the Performing Arts, Washington, D.C., "Film As/On Art," 1974; Centre National d'Art et de Culture Georges Pompidou, Paris, "Une Histoire du Cinéma," 1976; National Film Theater, London, "Structural Film Retrospective," 1976; The Museum of Modern Art, New York, "A History of the American Avant-Garde Cinema," 1976; FILMEX, Los Angeles, International Film Exposition, 1977; Whitney Museum of American Art, New York, New American Filmmakers Series, "Films Made through A.F.I. Grants," 1971, "Grain Fields," 1975, "Color Abstraction: Film," 1978; Whitney Museum of American Art, 1979 Biennial Exhibition.

Richard Shaw

Born in Hollywood, California, 1941
Studied at Orange Coast College, Costa Mesa, California (1961–63); San Francisco Art Institute (B.F.A., 1965); University of California, Davis (M.F.A., 1968)
Lives in Fairfax, California

Selected Solo Exhibitions: San Francisco Art Institute, 1967; Quay Gallery, San Francisco, 1970, 1971, 1973; San Francisco Museum of Art, 1973; Braunstein/Quay Gallery, New York, 1976; Braunstein/Quay Gallery, San Francisco, 1976; Braunstein Gallery, San Francisco, 1979; Allan Frumkin Gallery, New York, 1980.

Selected Group Exhibitions: Museum of Contemporary Crafts, New York, "New Ceramic Forms," 1965; National Collection of Fine Arts, Smithsonian Institution, Washington, D.C., "Objects U.S.A.," 1969; Whitney Museum of American Art, New York, "Annual Exhibition: Contemporary American Sculpture," 1970; The National Museum of Modern Art, Kyoto, Japan, "Contemporary Ceramic Art: Canada, U.S.A., Mexico, and Japan," 1971; Victoria and Albert Museum, London, "International Ceramics, 1972," 1972; San Francisco Museum of Art, "A Decade of Ceramic Art, 1962–1972: From the Collection of Professor and Mrs. Joseph Monsen," 1972; Whitney Museum of American Art, Downtown Branch, "Clay," 1974; San Francisco Museum of Modern Art, "Painting and Sculpture in California: The Modern Era," 1976 (traveled nationally); University of California, Davis, "Large Scale Ceramic Sculpture," 1979; Stedelijk Museum, Amsterdam, "West Coast Ceramics," 1979; Everson Museum of Art, Syracuse, New York, "A Century of Ceramics in the United States, 1878–1978," 1979–80 (traveled nationally); San Diego Museum of Art, California, "California Sculpture, 1975–1980," 1980.

Judith Shea

Born in Philadelphia, 1948
Studied at Parsons School of Design, New York (A.A., 1969); Parsons School of Design/The New School for Social Research, New York (B.F.A., 1975)
Lives in New York

Selected Solo Exhibitions: The Clocktower, Institute for Art and Urban Resources, New York, 1976; The Women's Center Gallery, New Haven, Connecticut, 1978; Willard Gallery, New York, 1980.

Selected Group Exhibitions: Artpark, Lewiston, New York, "Untailored Clothing," 1974; Artpark, "Making Clothes," 1975; Herbert F. Johnson Museum of Art, Cornell University, Ithaca, New York, "The Handwrought Object, 1776–1976," 1976; Moore College of Art, Philadelphia, "Collection in Progress: 200 or so Selections from the Collection of Milton Brutten and Helen Herrick," 1977; William Paterson College, Wayne, New Jersey, "The Fabric Workshop," 1978; Los Angeles Institute of Contemporary Art, "Clothing Constructions: An Exhibition of Artists Who Make Clothes," 1979; Amelie A. Wallace Gallery, State University of New York, College at Old Westbury, "Fabric into Art," 1980; Neuberger Museum, State University of New York, College at Purchase, "Seven Artists," 1980.

Stuart Sherman

Born in Providence, Rhode Island, 1945
Lives in New York

Sherman *(cont.)*

SELECTED SOLO EXHIBITIONS: Collective for Living Cinema, New York, 1979; Bleecker Street Cinema, New York, 1980; Anthology Film Archives, New York, 1980.

SELECTED GROUP EXHIBITIONS: Festival International de Jeune Cinéma, Hyères, France, 1979; Whitney Museum of American Art, New York, 1979 Biennial Exhibition.

Hollis Sigler

Born in Gary, Indiana, 1948
Studied at Moore College of Art, Philadelphia (B.F.A., 1970); School of The Art Institute of Chicago (M.F.A., 1973)
Lives in Chicago

SELECTED SOLO EXHIBITIONS: Nancy Lurie Gallery, Chicago, 1977, 1978; Rhode Island School of Design, Providence, 1979; Nancy Lurie Gallery, 1979; Gladstone-Villani Gallery, New York, 1979; Nancy Lurie Gallery, 1980; Barbara Gladstone Gallery, New York, 1980.

SELECTED GROUP EXHIBITIONS: The Art Institute of Chicago, "Artists of Chicago and Vicinity," 1973; Indianapolis Museum of Art, "Painting and Sculpture Today 1976," 1976; The Art Institute of Chicago, "Artists of Chicago and Vicinity," 1977, 1978; ARC Gallery, Chicago, "Narrative Imagery," 1979; Weatherspoon Art Gallery, University of North Carolina, Greensboro, "1980 Art on Paper," 1980; The Art Institute of Chicago, "Artists of Chicago and Vicinity," 1980.

Sandy Skoglund

Born in Boston, 1946
Studied at La Sorbonne and École du Louvre, Paris (1966–67); Smith College, Northampton, Massachusetts (B.A., 1968); University of Iowa, Iowa City (M.A., M.F.A., 1972); Summer Advanced Film Production Workshop, Institute of Film and Television, New York University (1975)
Lives in New York

SELECTED SOLO EXHIBITIONS: Joseloff Gallery, Hartford Art School of the University of Hartford, West Hartford, Connecticut, 1973; University of Connecticut, Torrington, 1975; Castelli Graphics, New York, 1980.

SELECTED GROUP EXHIBITIONS: Touchstone Gallery, New York, "Drawing II," 1978; Castelli Graphics, New York, "Pictures: Photographs," 1980; Barbara Gladstone Gallery, New York, "Interiors," 1980; Fogg Art Museum, Harvard University, Cambridge, Massachusetts, "Contemporary Photographs," 1980.

Alexis Smith

Born in Los Angeles, 1949
Studied at the University of California, Irvine (B.A., 1970)
Lives in Venice, California

SELECTED SOLO EXHIBITIONS: Riko Mizuno Gallery, Los Angeles, 1974; University of California, Santa Barbara, 1975; Whitney Museum of American Art, New York, 1975; Nicholas Wilder Gallery, Los Angeles, 1977; Holly Solomon Gallery, New York, 1977, 1978; Rosamund Felsen Gallery, Los Angeles, 1978; De Appel, Amsterdam, 1979; Holly Solomon Gallery, 1979, 1980; Rosamund Felsen Gallery, 1980.

SELECTED GROUP EXHIBITIONS: Pasadena Museum of Modern Art, California, "Southern California Attitudes," 1972; Whitney Museum of American Art, New York, 1975 Biennial Exhibition; Gallery of the School of Visual Arts, New York, "Four Los Angeles Artists: Foulkes, Goode, Smith, Wheeler," 1975 (traveled nationally); Sarah Lawrence College, Bronxville, New York, "Word, Image, Number," 1975; La Jolla Museum of Contemporary Art, California, "University of California at Irvine, 1965–75," 1975; Portland Center for the Visual Arts, Oregon, "Via Los Angeles," 1976; Los Angeles Institute of Contemporary Art, "Autobiographical Fantasies," 1976; Los Angeles Institute of Contemporary Art,

"Narrative Themes/Audio Works," 1977; Musée d'Art Moderne de la Ville de Paris, 10e Biennale de Paris, 1977; Contemporary Arts Museum, Houston, "American Narrative/Story Art, 1968–78," 1978 (traveled internationally); La Jolla Museum of Contemporary Art, "Southern California Styles of the 60s and 70s," 1978; Institute of Contemporary Art, Boston, "Narration," 1978; Whitney Museum of American Art, 1979 Biennial Exhibition.

Joan Snyder

Born in Highland Park, New Jersey, 1940
Studied at Douglass College, Rutgers University, New Brunswick, New Jersey (B.A., 1962); Rutgers University (M.F.A., 1966)
Lives in New York and Martins Creek, Pennsylvania

SELECTED SOLO EXHIBITIONS: University Art Gallery, Rutgers University, New Brunswick, New Jersey, 1966; Michael Walls Gallery, New York, 1971; Paley and Lowe Gallery, New York, 1971, 1973; Portland Center for the Visual Arts, Oregon, 1976; Hamilton Gallery, New York, 1978; Neuberger Museum, State University of New York, College at Purchase, 1978; San Francisco Art Institute, 1979.

SELECTED GROUP EXHIBITIONS: Whitney Museum of American Art, New York, "Annual Exhibition: Contemporary American Painting," 1972; Institute of Contemporary Art of The University of Pennsylvania, Philadelphia, "Grids," 1972; Whitney Museum of American Art, 1973 Biennial Exhibition; Whitney Museum of American Art, "American Drawings, 1963–1973," 1973; Corcoran Gallery of Art, Washington, D.C., "34th Biennial of Contemporary American Painting," 1975; The New Museum, New York, "The 1970's: New American Painting," 1979 (traveled internationally).

Robert Snyder

Born in Kalamazoo, Michigan, 1946
Studied at Indiana University, Bloomington (B.M., 1968);
Roosevelt University, Chicago (M.M., 1972)
Lives in Chicago

SELECTED GROUP EXHIBITIONS: The Museum of Modern Art, New York, "Open Circuits," 1974; Institute of Contemporary Art of The University of Pennsylvania, Philadelphia, "Video Art," 1975 (traveled nationally); Third International Computer Art Festival, New York, 1975; The Museum of Modern Art, New York, "Video Projects VI," 1975; Fourth International Computer Art Festival, New York, 1976; Computer Arts Exhibition, Tokyo, 1976, 1977; Everson Museum of Art, Syracuse, New York, "New Works in Abstract Video Imagery," 1976; The University of Michigan Museum of Art, Ann Arbor, "Chicago: The City and Its Artists," 1978; University of Chicago, "Video, the Meaning is the Use," 1978; Rome, "Video 79," 1979; Chicago Edition Center, "Videotape in Electronic Art," 1979; Anthology Film Archives, New York, "Video Series," 1979; Museum of Contemporary Art, Chicago, "Electronic Imagery," 1980.

Chick Strand

Born in San Francisco, 1931
Studied at the University of California, Berkeley (B.A., 1961); University of California, Los Angeles (M.F.A., 1971)
Lives in Tujunga, California

SELECTED SOLO EXHIBITIONS: Independent Film Oasis of Los Angeles, 1976; Canyon Cinematheque, San Francisco, 1976; Pacific Film Archive, University Art Museum, Berkeley, California, 1976; The Museum of Modern Art, New York, 1976; Film Forum, New York, 1976; Pasadena Film Forum, California, 1976; Millennium Film Workshop, New York, 1978; Museum of Art, Carnegie Institute, Pittsburgh, 1978; Independent Film Oasis of Los Angeles, 1979; Bellas Artes, San Miguel de Allende, Mexico, 1979; Image, Atlanta, 1979; Pasadena Film Forum, 1980; Sheldon Memorial Art Gallery, University of Nebraska, Lincoln, 1980; Canyon Cinematheque, 1980; Joslyn Art Museum, Omaha, Nebraska, 1980; San Jose Museum of Art, California, 1980; Stedelijk Museum, Amsterdam, 1980; London Filmmakers Cooperative, 1980.

Strand *(cont.)*

Selected Group Exhibitions: New York Film Festival, 1969; Whitney Museum of American Art, New York, New American Filmmakers Series, "Films by Women," 1971; FILMEX, Los Angeles International Film Exposition, 1971; Women's Film Festival, New York, 1974, 1976; FILMEX, Los Angeles International Film Exposition, 1976; Iran Film Festival, Teheran, 1977; London Experimental Film Festival, 1979.

Wayne Thiebaud

Born in Mesa, Arizona, 1920
Studied at Sacramento State College, California (B.A., 1951; M.A., 1952)
Lives in Sacramento and San Francisco

Selected Solo Exhibitions: E.B. Crocker Art Gallery, Sacramento, California, 1950; Staempfli Gallery, New York, 1960; Allan Stone Gallery, New York, 1962; University Art Museum, Stanford University, California, 1965 (traveled nationally); Pasadena Art Museum, California, 1968 (traveled nationally); Whitney Museum of American Art, New York, 1971 (traveled nationally); The Art Institute of Chicago, 1972; Portland Center for the Visual Arts, Oregon, 1973; Stedelijk Van Abbemuseum, Eindhoven, Holland, 1973.

Selected Group Exhibitions: Los Angeles Art Association Galleries, "Artists Under Thirty-three," 1949 (traveled nationally); Pasadena Art Museum, California, "New Paintings of Common Objects," 1962; Sidney Janis Gallery, New York, "The New Realists," 1962; Haags Gemeentemuseum, The Hague, "Nieuwe Realisten," 1964; Whitney Museum of American Art, New York, "Annual Exhibition: Contemporary American Painting," 1967; 34th Venice Biennale, 1968; Institute of Contemporary Art of The University of Pennsylvania, Philadelphia, "The Highway," 1970; Kassel, West Germany, Documenta 5, 1972.

Richard Thompson

Born in McMinnville, Oregon, 1945
Studied at Oregon State University, Corvallis (1963–65); University of New Mexico, Albuquerque (B.F.A., 1971; M.A., 1972)
Lives in Albuquerque, New Mexico

Selected Solo Exhibitions: Jonson Gallery, The University of New Mexico, Albuquerque, 1974; Gallery of Visual Arts, University of Montana, Missoula, 1975; Hill's Gallery, Santa Fe, New Mexico, 1975; Harlan Gallery, Tucson, Arizona, 1977; Tyler Museum of Art, Tyler, Texas, 1978 (traveled nationally); Warehouse Living Arts Center, Corsicana, Texas, 1979; Space, Los Angeles, 1980.

Selected Group Exhibitions: Museum of New Mexico, Santa Fe, "Southwest Biennial," 1972; Museum of New Mexico, "New Mexico Biennial," 1973; Whitney Museum of American Art, New York, 1975 Biennial Exhibition; Joslyn Art Museum, Omaha, Nebraska, "Midwest Biennial," 1976; Museum of New Mexico, "Made in New Mexico," 1977; Art Museum, University of New Mexico, Albuquerque, "Current Work," 1977; Museum of New Mexico, "Southwest Biennial," 1978; Museum of Albuquerque, "Albuquerque Artists II," 1978; Downtown Center for the Arts, Albuquerque, "Provocations/Regenerations," 1979; Fruit Market Gallery, Edinburgh, "New New Mexico," 1980.

Joan Thorne

Born in New York, 1943
Studied at New York University (B.A., 1965); Hunter College, New York (M.A., 1968)
Lives in New York

Selected Solo Exhibitions: Corcoran Gallery of Art, Washington, D.C., 1973; Fischbach Gallery, New York, 1974; The Clocktower, Institute for Art and Urban Resources, New York, 1979; Willard Gallery, New York, 1980.

Selected Group Exhibitions: Whitney Museum of American Art, New York, "Annual Exhibition: Contemporary American Painting," 1972; Loeb Center, New York University, "Five Painters," 1973; Institute of Contemporary Art of The

University of Pennsylvania, Philadelphia, "Eight Abstract Painters," 1978; Renaissance Society at the University of Chicago, "Thick Paint," 1978; Grey Art Gallery, New York University, "American Painting: The Eighties," 1979 (traveled internationally); Grand Palais, Paris, "L'Amérique aux Indépendants," 1980.

Jack Tworkov

Born in Biala, Poland, 1900
Studied at Columbia College of Columbia University, New York (1920–23); The Art Students League of New York (1925–26)
Lives in New York and Provincetown, Massachusetts

SELECTED SOLO EXHIBITIONS: ACA Galleries, New York, 1940; Egan Gallery, New York, 1947; The Baltimore Museum of Art, 1948; Egan Gallery, 1949, 1952, 1954; Walker Art Center, Minneapolis, 1957; Stable Gallery, New York, 1957, 1958, 1959; Leo Castelli Gallery, New York, 1961, 1963; Whitney Museum of American Art, New York, 1965 (traveled nationally); The Toledo Museum of Art, Ohio, 1971; French & Company, New York, 1972; Portland Center for the Visual Arts, Oregon, 1974; The Denver Art Museum, 1974; Contemporary Arts Center, Cincinnati, 1975; Nancy Hoffman Gallery, New York, 1975, 1977; Third Eye Centre, Glasgow, 1979–80 (traveled internationally).

SELECTED GROUP EXHIBITIONS: Kassel, West Germany, Documenta 2, 1958; The Museum of Modern Art, New York, "New American Painting," 1958 (traveled internationally); Whitney Museum of American Art, New York, 1973 Biennial Exhibition; The Solomon R. Guggenheim Museum, New York, "Aspects of Postwar Painting in America," 1976; Hirshhorn Museum and Sculpture Garden, Smithsonian Institution, Washington, D.C., "Artist-Immigrants of America, 1876–1976," 1976; The Art Institute of Chicago, "Drawings of the 70's," 1977.

William Viola

Born in Flushing, New York, 1951
Studied at the College of Visual and Performing Arts, Syracuse University, Syracuse, New York (B.F.A., 1973)
Lives in New York

SELECTED SOLO EXHIBITIONS: Anthology Film Archives, New York, 1975; Zona, Florence, 1975; Long Beach Museum of Art, California, 1975; Everson Museum of Art, Syracuse, New York, 1975; Vehicle Art, Montreal, 1975; The Kitchen Center for Video, Music and Dance, New York, 1977; The Museum of Modern Art, New York, 1980.

SELECTED GROUP EXHIBITIONS: John F. Kennedy Center for the Performing Arts, Washington, D.C., "Art Now, '74," 1974; Whitney Museum of American Art, New York, 1975 Biennial Exhibition; San Francisco Museum of Modern Art, "Video Art—An Overview," 1976; Musée d'Art Moderne de la Ville de Paris, 1977 Biennale; The Museum of Modern Art, New York, "Project," 1978; Whitney Museum of American Art, 1979 Biennial Exhibition.

Russ Warren

Born in Washington, D.C., 1951
Studied at the University of St. Thomas, Houston (1969–71); University of New Mexico, Albuquerque (B.F.A., 1973); University of Texas, San Antonio (M.F.A., 1977)
Lives in Davidson, North Carolina

SELECTED SOLO EXHIBITIONS: New Orleans Museum of Art, 1976; San Antonio Museum of Modern Art, 1976; Art Gallery, Davidson College, Davidson, North Carolina, 1979; University of North Carolina, Charlotte, 1980.

SELECTED GROUP EXHIBITIONS: New Orleans Museum of Art, "1975 Artists Biennial," 1975; Amarillo Art Center, Amarillo, Texas, "Amarillo Competition," 1977; The Southeastern Center for Contemporary Art, Winston-Salem, North Carolina, "47th Southeastern Competition for Paintings and Sculpture," 1979; Mint Museum of Art, Charlotte, North Carolina, 1979 Biennial; North Carolina Museum

Warren *(cont.)*

of Art, Raleigh, "1980 North Carolina Annual," 1980; New Orleans Museum of Art, "1980 New Orleans Triennial," 1980; Southeastern Center for Contemporary Art, "48th Southeastern Competition for Drawing, Photography and Printmaking," 1980.

William Wegman

Born in Holyoke, Massachusetts, 1942
Studied at the Massachusetts College of Art, Boston (B.F.A., 1964); University of Illinois, Champaign-Urbana (M.F.A., 1967)
Lives in New York

SELECTED SOLO EXHIBITIONS: Galerie Sonnabend, Paris, 1971; Konrad Fischer Gallery, Düsseldorf, West Germany, 1972; Los Angeles County Museum of Art, 1973; The Kitchen Center for Video, Music and Dance, New York, 1976; Holly Solomon Gallery, New York, 1979; University of Colorado Art Galleries, Boulder, 1980 (traveled nationally).

SELECTED GROUP EXHIBITIONS: Museum of Contemporary Art, Chicago, "Art by Telephone," 1969; The Detroit Institute of Arts, "Other Ideas," 1969; Whitney Museum of American Art, New York, 1973 Biennial Exhibition; Wadsworth Atheneum, Hartford, Connecticut, "Matrix 9," 1975; Museum of Contemporary Art, Chicago, "The Word As Image," 1977; Santa Barbara Museum of Art, California, "Attitudes: Photography in the 1970's," 1979.

Robert Wilson

Born in Waco, Texas, 1941
Studied at the University of Texas, Austin (1959–65); Pratt Institute, Brooklyn, New York (B.F.A., 1965); Arcosanti Community, Arizona (apprentice to Paolo Soleri, 1966)
Lives in New York

SELECTED SOLO EXHIBITIONS: Willard Gallery, New York, 1971; Musée Galliera, Paris, 1972; Galerie Wünsche, Bonn, West Germany, 1975; The Kitchen Center for Video, Music and Dance, New York, 1976 (video performance); Iolas Gallery, New York, 1976; Multiples/Marian Goodman Gallery, New York, 1977; Paula Cooper Gallery, New York, 1978; Galerie Rudolf Zwirner, Cologne, West Germany, 1979; Multiples/Marian Goodman Gallery, 1979; Contemporary Arts Center, Cincinnati, 1980 (traveled nationally).

SELECTED THEATER PERFORMANCES: Brooklyn Academy of Music Opera House, New York, *The Life and Times of Sigmund Freud*, 1969; University Theatre, Iowa City, *Deafman Glance*, 1970 (traveled internationally); Det Ny Theatre, Copenhagen, *The Life and Times of Joseph Stalin*, 1973 (traveled internationally); Teatro Caio Melisso, Spoleto, Italy, *A Letter for Queen Victoria*, 1974 (traveled internationally); Brooklyn Academy of Music Opera House, New York, *$ Value of Man*, 1975; Festival d'Avignon, France, *Einstein on the Beach*, 1976 (traveled internationally); Quirk Auditorium, Eastern Michigan University, Ypsilanti, *I Was Sitting On My Patio This Guy Appeared I Thought I Was Hallucinating*, 1977 (traveled internationally); Schaubühne am Halleschen Ufer, West Berlin, *Death Destruction and Detroit*, 1979; Lion Theatre, New York, *Edison*, 1979 (traveled internationally).

Robert Zakanitch

Born in Elizabeth, New Jersey, 1935
Studied at Newark School of Fine and Industrial Art, New Jersey (1955–57)
Lives in New York

SELECTED SOLO EXHIBITIONS: Stable Gallery, New York, 1968; Cunningham Ward, New York, 1973, 1974; Holly Solomon Gallery, New York, 1977; Robert Miller Gallery, New York, 1978; Galerie Rudolf Zwirner, Cologne, West Germany, 1979; Robert Miller Gallery, 1979, 1980.

SELECTED GROUP EXHIBITIONS: Whitney Museum of American Art, New York, "Annual Exhibition: Contemporary American Painting," 1968; Whitney Museum of American Art, "Annual Exhibition: Contemporary American Painting," 1969; Whitney Museum of American Art, "Structure of Color," 1971; Corcoran Gallery of

Art, Washington, D.C., "Thirty-third Biennial Exhibition of Contemporary American Painting," 1973; Alessandra Gallery, New York, "Ten Approaches to the Decorative," 1976; P.S. 1, Institute for Art and Urban Resources, Long Island City, New York, "Pattern Painting," 1977; Institute of Contemporary Art of The University of Pennsylvania, Philadelphia, "The Decorative Impulse," 1979; Mannheimer Kunstverein, Mannheim, West Germany, "Dekor," 1980 (traveled internationally); 39th Venice Biennale, 1980.